W9-ANC-859

Open for Debate

Cloning

Open for Debate

Cloning

Lila Perl

Marshall Cavendish
Benchmark
New York

With thanks to Mark Westhusin, associate professor at the College of Veterinary Medicine, Texas A&M University, for his expert review of this manuscript.

Marshall Cavendish Benchmark
99 White Plains Road
Tarrytown, NY 10591
www.marshallcavendish.us

All Internet sites were available and accurate when sent to press.

Library of Congress Cataloging-in-Publication Data
Perl, Lila.
Cloning / by Lila Perl.—1st ed.
p. cm.—(Open for debate)
Includes bibliographical references and index.
ISBN 0-7614-1884-9
1. Cloning. 2. Cloning—Social aspects. I. Title. II. Series.
QH442.2.P468 2004
176—dc22
2004021813

Photo research by Linda Sykes Picture Research, Inc., Hilton Head, SC

Ronnen Eshel/Corbis: cover, 1, 2-3, 5, 123; Universal/The Kobal Collection: 6; Najah Feanny/Corbis
Saba: 13; McPherson Colin/ Corbis Sygma: 18; Jeffrey Markowitz/Corbis Sygma: 27;
Adrian Arbeb/Corbis: 33; Reuters/Corbis: 38, 52, 60, 106; Archivo Iconografico, S. A./Corbis: 44;
Frank Trapper/Corbis: 54; Lester Lefkowitz/Corbis: 62; Kim Kyung-Hoon/Reuters/Corbis: 64; Roger
Ressmeyer/Corbis: 74; Ted Spiegel/Corbis: 79; Corbis Sygma: 86, 88; Images.com/Corbis: 96; Corbis:
99; Pascal Parrot/Corbis Sygma: 112; Manuela Hartling/Corbis: 120.

Printed in China

135642

Contents

MARY SHELLEY'S NOVEL *FRANKENSTEIN* HAS RECEIVED MANY STAGE AND SCREEN ADAPTATIONS. THIS POSTER IS FROM THE **1931** MOVIE VERSION.

Foreword

Nearly two hundred years before it became scientifically possible, writers of fanciful fiction began teasing us with the prospect of creating human life in the laboratory rather than in the human body. The classic tale of a manmade man was Mary Shelley's *Frankenstein*, written in 1818 in England as a cautionary fable that was intended to warn us of the danger of playing God.

In Mary Shelley's novel, the mad scientist Dr. Frankenstein creates a manlike creature that turns out to be a rampaging monster. Frankenstein's monster kills a number of people and eventually destroys Dr. Frankenstein himself. This is the penalty one must pay, the author tells us, for attempting to violate the grand design of nature.

Fast forward to the year 1978 in the United States. On March 31, the purportedly true story of an aging multimillionaire, who had a newborn copy of himself created through laboratory science, appeared in bookstores. The book, which was accepted as nonfiction and soon climbed the bestseller lists, was written by a former journalist named David Rorvik. Its title was *In His Image: The Cloning of a Man*.

Here was no patched-together, awkward, stumbling version of the full-grown human form, as described in Mary Shelley's *Frankenstein.* Rorvik's claim was that the human image that had been created was a newborn infant whose genetic makeup was identical to that of the adult male multimillionaire. Having desired an ideal heir to his fortune, the older man was now provided with a carbon copy of himself but one that was young enough to outlive him for many years.

In other words, the scientific marvel that had been created, according to Rorvik, was a clone—an exact duplicate of a living thing. A clone has the very same genes, or units of hereditary information, which its parent has, and would therefore have all of the same characteristics, from the color and texture of its hair to the shape and growth tendencies of its toenails.

It would also have the same organs, tissues, and other physical features and capacities of the human being from which it had been cloned. This would be true because it had been grown, presumably, from the nucleus of a parent cell and contained the same chromosomes, or specific bearers of genetic information.

The scientific establishment of 1978 was rocked by the claim that a human being had been successfully cloned. At the time, cell biologists had managed to clone such life forms as frogs but were still having difficulties cloning mice, to say nothing of other mammals. Soon a barrage of demands for scientific proof of the birth of a human clone descended on Rorvik and his prominent and heretofore reputable book publisher.

Within a short time, a British scientist working in the field of embryology instituted a defamation suit, asserting that Rorvik had inappropriately and without permission used his research in the book as technical backup. The defamation suit went to court. Rorvik and his publisher not only lost the case but his book was pronounced by the court to be "a hoax and a fraud."

But even as he paid the price in professional integrity, book earnings, and legal expenses, Rorvik stuck to his story. Yet, as the truth became known, many found further proof of Rorvik's deception. He had chosen to publish *In His Image* on March 31, the eve of April Fool's Day—the traditional date for the dissemination of gigantic jokes.

While cloning as a means of creating people remained a distant if not impossible prospect in the late 1970s, laboratory technologies had already been developed to assist in human sexual reproduction. They included artificial insemination (AI) and in vitro fertilization (IVF).

In AI, sperm is introduced via a laboratory technique into the female reproductive tract. In IVF, sperm is introduced into the egg under laboratory conditions in a glass or plastic receptacle [in vitro = in glass] in order to bring about fertilization. The fertilized egg is then implanted in the uterus of the natural mother or, if that presents a problem, a surrogate mother who can carry the baby to term for its genetic parents.

The first "test-tube" baby (as the early creations of IVF were known) was Louise Brown, born in England in 1978—the same year that *In His Image* was published. Many people frowned on the interference of science in the process of human procreation because of their religious beliefs and ethical and moral principles. But at least the sexual joining of sperm and egg to create a new life was in keeping with the laws of nature. What was really abhorrent to adherents of the traditional view of reproduction was the asexual nature of human cloning, which required only one parent, who could be either male or female. So it was a relief to learn in the late 1970s that human cloning was merely a product of the imaginations of fraudulent nonfiction authors, science fiction writers, and Hollywood moviemakers.

In the years that followed, however, a group of animal scientists had quietly moved on in pursuit of the cloning of mammals, not laboratory mice but large farm animals such as sheep, cows, and pigs. Their reasons were pragmatic rather than experimental, for their goal was to produce cloned agricultural stock for use in industry.

It was as a result of this effort that on July 5, 1996, the first large mammal to be cloned from an adult animal—Dolly the sheep—was born at a research center in Scotland known as the Roslin Institute.

The method used to clone Dolly was eerily reminiscent of the one presumably used in the creation of a human clone in David Rorvik's discredited book *In His Image*. A mature cell from a chosen parent—in Dolly's case a mammary cell from a Finn-Dorset sheep—had its nucleus transferred to an emptied-out, or enucleated, egg cell that was then implanted in the uterus of a surrogate mother sheep. In Rorvik's book, a cell taken from the body of "Max," the multimillionaire, was transferred to a donated egg that was implanted in the uterus of a beautiful sixteen-year-old virgin and surrogate mother called "Sparrow," whom "Max" had chosen to bring his child to term.

Just as newborn Dolly was in every way a genetic replica of her Finn-Dorset sheep mother, "Max's" presumed child was an exact newborn genetic copy of his multimillionaire father. Neither offspring had resulted from the mating of a male and a female. Both clones had been produced in a laboratory and both had been produced asexually. "Max's" cloned offspring was fiction. But Dolly was a real live clone. With her birth, it appeared that fiction had become fact and the laws of nature had been broken forever.

Most serious was the implicit suggestion that if a sheep could be cloned by transferring the nucleus of one cell into another, more than likely a human being could be, too. So it was not surprising that the excitement that greeted the announcement of Dolly's birth was almost immediately tempered by alarm at the prospects for humanity. In the imaginations of some people, human clones were suddenly everywhere, overtaking society, enslaving the non-clones, and eventually ruling the world. Scenarios of every sort ran rampant.

The scientific community, too, was deeply stirred by the news of Dolly's birth. "It's unbelievable," said Lee Silver, a molecular biologist at Princeton University. "It basically means that there are no limits. It means that all of science fiction is true."

Dolly's birth was kept secret for more than seven months, from July 1996 to February 1997, and was announced in *The New York Times* for the first time on February 23. True, Dolly was only a sheep. However, the debate on human cloning was about to begin with a vengeance.

1

A Human Clone in Sheep's Clothing?

It was understandable that the announcement, on February 23, 1997, of the existence of a healthy seven-month-old cloned sheep should have fired up the imaginations of the press, the public, and even the scientific community. For, on the surface at least, Dolly—the first sheep to be cloned from the cell of an adult animal—appeared to be the prototype for the first human clone. How soon would it be, following the same method used by the animal scientists at the Roslin Institute, before the first human baby cloned from the cell of a human adult would take its place among us?

For a possible answer to that question, it was necessary to take a closer look at the creation of Dolly—its background, its purpose, the details of the process of transferring nuclei from one living cell to another, and the difficulties encountered along the way.

DR. IAN WILMUT SITS WITH DOLLY, THE FIRST SHEEP TO BE CLONED FROM THE CELL OF AN ADULT ANIMAL.

The Story Behind the Story of Dolly

At the time of Dolly's birth, Ian Wilmut, a mammalian embryologist, was the leader of the Roslin Institute team that, since the late 1980s, had been conducting experiments on cloning sheep and other large farm animals for the purpose of producing "living drug factories." In other words, the scientists at Roslin, working in conjunction with a small Scottish company known as PPL Therapeutics (Pharmaceutical Proteins, Limited), had been trying to develop a means of incorporating curative substances for human illnesses into the milk of sheep and cows.

Wilmut and others had already succeeded in introducing into sheep the human gene for the blood-clotting protein to treat hemophilia in humans. Hemophilia is a human genetic defect, chiefly affecting males, in which bleeding to death even from muscular strains, to say nothing of open cuts and wounds, is a serious hazard. So being able to produce flocks of sheep whose milk contained the important clotting factors VIII and IX meant that there would be an increased supply of the medicine (which is extracted from the milk) for hemophiliacs. There was only one guaranteed way, however, to procreate animals capable of delivering the life-saving drug. It was to produce clones from parents who already possessed the human clotting gene, which had resulted from the transgenic modification of cells—the introduction of genes from one species into another.

Long before Dolly, embryologists had been attempting to clone vertebrate animals and they reported their first, although only partial, success with frogs as early as 1952. But their method and that of many cell biologists who followed them was to work with embryos, or clusters of newly fertilized cells in the very first stages of development. By dividing the embryos and transferring their nuclei into enucleated, unfertilized eggs that were then implanted into the female of the species, they were able to make genetic copies, or clones, of mice, sheep, and cows.

In 1995, the year before Dolly was born, Wilmut and his partner, Keith Campbell, produced twin lambs named Megan and Morag from cells derived from embryos. But so far no clone had been created from an adult body cell, also known as a somatic cell in order to distinguish it from an adult germ cell such as an egg or a sperm.

Following the births of Megan and Morag, Davor Solter, a Croatian biologist who had come to the United States in 1973, and who had written in the mid-1980s that he believed the cloning of mammals to be impossible, admitted to the success of embryonic animal cloning. But he warned, in an article in *Nature* published in March 1996, that, "Cloning animals from adult cells will be considerably harder." Within months, Wilmut and Campbell were to prove that cloning a mammal from an adult somatic cell rather than embryonic cells was after all possible.

Dolly's mother, as it turned out, had been a six-year-old pregnant Finn-Dorset ewe, who was no longer even alive at the time of Dolly's birth. Because of the active and fast-growing nature of mammary cells in pregnant animals, Wilmut and Campbell chose that type of somatic cell to see if they could produce an offspring that would be a genetic copy of its parent.

The two animal scientists began their experiment by freezing a large number of parental mammary cells. Their nuclear-transfer procedure was as follows. Two cells were used. The recipient was an unfertilized egg cell (with its own nucleus removed) that had resulted from the ovulation of a female of the species. The donor cell was, in this case, an adult mammary cell containing the genetic material of the parent animal.

As described by Wilmut, "A researcher working under a high-power microscope holds the recipient egg cell by suction on the end of a fine pipette and uses an extremely fine micropipette to suck out the chromosomes." The nucleus of the donor cell is thus injected into the enucleated egg and, usually through stimulation by an electric pulse, the fused cells begin to develop into an embryo that can be implanted into the uterus of a surrogate mother sheep.

Dolly's surrogate mother was a Scottish Blackface mountain ewe, a different variety of sheep from her genetic mother, and one with which she had no hereditary traits in common. At birth Dolly had the appearance of a perfectly ordinary Finn-Dorset sheep. She weighed 14.5 pounds (6.6 kilograms), and seemed to be normal and healthy in every way.

Statistically, however, Dolly was a standout. She was the only live birth to result from 277 attempts at cell fusion that had taken place at the Roslin Institute. Of those attempts, only 29 of the fused cells had begun to divide to become embryos. All 29 embryos were then implanted in female sheep. But only 13 sheep became pregnant, and most of the pregnancies resulted in miscarriages. Only one live lamb was born—Dolly.

Grahame Bulfield, director and chief executive of the Roslin Institute, admitted to the low success rate of the first experiment with cloning from an adult cell rather than from embryonic cells, "We don't know," Bulfield remarked, "if that was unlucky and we could get that rate higher, as we have done with the embryo cells. We don't know that it wasn't a lucky one out of 277. Maybe the true rate is one out of 10,000."

Success rates with mammals cloned from adult cells have improved somewhat since Wilmut's first try with Dolly. But they are still a long way from the high percentage rate that would be hoped for in human cloning, and the risk factors remain enormous. While Wilmut admitted in 1997 that it was theoretically possible that humans could be cloned using the same methods by which Dolly was created, he made it clear that such an undertaking would be "offensive" and an outcome that he hoped would never come to pass.

What was, and continues to be, remarkable about the cloning of even one live birth from an adult cell is that such cells were previously believed to be incapable of producing a replica of an entire animal. This was because adult cells, as opposed to early embryonic cells, are differentiated. That is to say, they have acquired specific characteristics in order to perform particular functions in the organism.

While early embryonic cells are undifferentiated (capable of developing into any type of body cell, or totipotent), adult cells are mature and have narrower functions. Dolly's mother's mammary cell was one example of an adult, differentiated cell. Other examples of adult cells include those that make up the blood, brain, muscle, skin, and other organs and tissues of the body. Yet, Dolly's birth proved that an entire genetic copy, a clone, could be created from an adult animal cell.

A Glossary of Genetic Terms

cell the basic unit or building block of a living organism, capable of dividing and duplicating throughout life

chromosome threadlike structure in the nucleus of a cell that consists of strands of DNA, the nucleic acid that bears hereditary information

clone a genetic copy of a living thing; a clone is a product of asexual reproduction

DNA deoxyribonucleic acid, the chemical from which a cell's genetic material is made, containing the substances adenine, guanine, cytosine, and thymine; James D. Watson and Francis Crick unraveled the structure of DNA in 1953 and received the Nobel Prize in 1962 for their discovery

differentiated describes cells that have acquired specific functions, such as making up the blood, skin, muscle, or other tissues in a living organism

egg cell a mature female germ, or reproductive, cell that is ready for fertilization

embryo group of living cells in an animal or human in the earliest stage of development

fertilization fusion of mature egg cell and spermatozoon, or sperm cell, for the purpose of sexual reproduction

gene unit of hereditary information, or sets of instructions in the cells, made up of DNA

genome all the units of hereditary information in a representative member of a given species of living organism

nucleus part of a cell that contains its genetic material, or chromosomes

totipotent undifferentiated, embryonic cells that are capable of developing into any type of cell in a living organism

How was this done? As explained by Arlene Judith Klotzko in *The Cloning Sourcebook*, "In essence, the Roslin team had to trick the adult cell's DNA into reverting to its undifferentiated past by placing the mammary cells in a culture and starving them of nutrients for several days. In this quiescent state, few if any genes remained switched on. When the nuclei were removed from the adult cells, placed next to the enucleated egg cells, and fused by electricity, the eggs were able to reprogram the donor nuclei into behaving as if they had come from undifferentiated cells."

The cloning of the twin sheep Megan and Morag in 1995, the year before Dolly was born, was an important step

THE ROSLIN INSTITUTE HAS EXPERIMENTED WITH "LIVING DRUG FACTORIES" IN THE FORM OF CHICKENS CAPABLE OF PRODUCING EGG PROTEINS TO TREAT CANCER.

in the successful use of differentiated cells. For, unlike the previous cloning of sheep and cows from early embryonic cells, Wilmut and Campbell had used fetal cells, a *mature* form of embryonic cells, which were already differentiated but which they had rendered into a state of quiescence, or inactivity. Yet, to the press and the public, it was the birth of Dolly that appeared to be the real breakthrough.

The reason was obvious. Cloning a human from an embryo, either undifferentiated and totipotent, or mature and differentiated, was abhorrent. It would mean destroying a human life in the making. If, however, a human could be cloned from a skin, muscle, mammary, or other cell of a mature adult, human cloning was indeed a possibility.

The Creators of Dolly Discuss Human Cloning

In the weeks following the February 23, 1997, announcement of Dolly's existence, newspapers and magazines in the United States made an almost instant leap from descriptions of the celebrated sheep to discussions of human cloning. *Newsweek*, in its issue dated March 10, 1997, put three identical human babies enclosed in glass laboratory beakers on its front cover, indicating that the era of human cloning was already on the horizon. *Time* magazine wondered in its issue of the same date, "Will We Follow the Sheep?" To make the prospect of human cloning understandable, a variety of newsstand publications explained and diagrammed the process of adult-cell nuclear transfer for the public.

In the United Kingdom, the land of Dolly's birth, there was a similar outburst of enthusiasm and speculation. *The Daily Mail* newspaper headlined its February 24 issue with the question of whether even the cells of deceased human beings would lend themselves to cloning, with the headline, "Could We Now Raise the Dead?"

The Birth of Polly and the Death of Dolly

At Roslin, the work of creating "living drug factories," otherwise known as "pharming" (the production of pharmaceuticals by inserting human disease-fighting genes or enzymes into farm animals) continued. In July 1997, a successor to Dolly named Polly—because she was a Poll Dorset lamb—was born. Polly had been genetically engineered to contain a human gene in every cell of her body, a modification that would make her and those animals that followed in her pattern capable of delivering drugs for the treatment of human ills even more efficient.

Unlike Dolly (but like Megan and Morag), Polly had been created from specially treated fetal cells—sheep cells that had grown past the embryo stage into that of the early formation of the organism. The nuclear-transfer method had also been used. There were, however, no plans at the time of the birth of Polly to clone any more sheep from adult cells.

One of the hazards of cloning individuals—animal or human—from adult cells may be the factor of premature aging. In any case, after having been mated and having produced a number of lambs, Dolly developed a lung disease common in older sheep as well as signs of arthritis, and had to be put down in February 2003. Dolly was only seven-and-a-half years old and had lived roughly half of a sheep's normal life span.

One explanation is as follows. As cells get old, their telomeres—the repeated units of DNA at the ends of the chromosomes in their nuclei—start to break down. Dolly's telomeres, when examined, were shown to be shorter than in sheep of a similar age. Was this because Dolly had been derived from the adult cell of a six-year-old parent sheep? Did this indicate that at the age of one Dolly was already age seven? And what might this mean for the life spans of any future human clones created from the cells of adults who were already in their mature years? On a final note regarding Dolly, after a full postmortem—and as reported at the time of her death in 2003—the famous sheep was to be stuffed and put on display in the National Museum of Scotland in Edinburgh.

During the spring and summer of 1997, the creators of Dolly at the Roslin Institute were asked to respond to the assumptions about the imminence of human cloning that had greeted their achievement.

The purpose of their experiments had, of course, had nothing to do with facilitating the replication of human beings. It had been to produce transgenic animals (animals implanted with certain human genes) that could secrete pharmaceutical compounds in their milk. Following their work with the introduction of the human clotting factor in sheep's milk, the purification of which resulted in a drug to treat hemophiliacs, the Roslin scientists had altered sheep's genes to produce another disease-fighting drug—alpha-1 antitrypsin.

This drug could be used to treat victims of the genetic disease cystic fibrosis, in which abnormally thick mucus is secreted and settles in the lungs and other organs. Treatment with alpha-1 antitrypsin—produced via Roslin's "living drug factories"—has helped to prolong the lives of cystic fibrosis sufferers, most of whom previously died in childhood or in their early teens.

When asked about his view on the subject of human cloning, Roslin Institute director Bulfield replied, "The general view that we have taken on the cloning of human beings is a fivefold stance. First, we don't know whether we can do it on humans. Second, we have no intention of doing it on humans. Third, we don't believe that there is any justified clinical reason for doing it on humans. Fourth, we have no intention of licensing our technology for anybody to do it on humans. Fifth, it is illegal, at least in Britain."

Wilmut and Campbell held similarly negative views. Wilmut said, "I am uncomfortable with copying people, because that would involve not treating them as individuals." Campbell replied, "Human cloning—obviously this was bound to raise its head. Personally and medically, I see no reasons for cloning humans to term. I am against using nuclear transfer to produce humans. Full stop!"

Clearly, the Roslin animal scientists saw many drawbacks to the idea of human cloning. Even if it were technically feasible, Bulfield estimated that "the cloning of one human being could well require the use of 1,000 eggs and 20 to 50 surrogate mothers."

2

Why Create Copies of Ourselves?

In spite of the negative views of human cloning expressed by the Roslin scientists following the birth of Dolly, the prospect of creating genetic copies of human beings fired the imaginations of people around the world. They included molecular biologists, specialists in the field of human fertility, physicians, social thinkers, and dreamers and visionaries with pseudo-scientific backgrounds, as well as ordinary men and women.

The technical capability for cloning a human being had perhaps not yet arrived, but that did not deter the pro-cloning faction from declaring itself in favor of it. Even those who opposed human cloning agreed that it was destined to happen in the very near future.

Kenneth M. Boyd, a medical ethicist at the University of Edinburgh, reluctantly admitted in the wake of Dolly that nuclear transfer technology "*could* eventually be used to clone not just human tissues or organs, but also individual human beings. Why should this *not* be done? Behind this question is the suspicion, even the conviction, that eventually it *will* be done. Scientific curiosity, or the prospect of profits to be made, will be too compelling to resist."

Among the most curious and even anxious of the pro-cloning advocates is Richard Dawkins, a British sociobiologist who was among the first to declare that he was strongly in favor of having himself cloned. The reason Dawkins offered was that "it would be mind-bogglingly fascinating to watch a younger edition of myself growing up in the twenty-first century instead of the 1940s."

Dawkins elaborated on this theme in writings for two London newspapers in 1997. "Mightn't even you, in your heart of hearts, quite like to be cloned?" he asked his readers. "My feeling is founded on pure curiosity. I know how I turned out, having been born in the 1940s, schooled in the 1950s, come of age in the 1960s, and so on." Watching a fifty-years-younger copy of himself, Dawkins mused, would be like turning back the clock to his own youth, and would give him an opportunity to point out to his junior copy where he had gone wrong and how his mistakes could be avoided.

Some opponents of cloning might wonder if curiosity about a younger version of oneself is a good enough reason to run all the risks (including the possibilities of premature aging of the clone as well as incidences of genetic mutations and malformations) involved in creating a genetic copy of a fifty-year-old man? They might even accuse Dawkins of revealing a certain amount of arrogance in wanting a youthful subject to correct and to direct on the path of life?

Also, Dawkins' clone might have his parent's DNA via nuclear cell transfer. But once it had reached the early embryonic stage and been implanted in a surrogate mother, its uterine environment would be very different from the one that nurtured Dawkins fifty years earlier.

Even more drastic changes would take place once the period of gestation was completed. Dawkins's clone would emerge into an environment that was physically, culturally, socially, economically, politically, and emotionally immensely changed from the one that Dawkins had been born into fifty years earlier. So, in many ways, a clone is a genetic copy with numerous influences that show us the potential power of nurture over nature, or at least gives us a means of studying the two. Even naturally reproduced genetically identical twins, who share so many more facets of their environment, are not exact copies of one another, as has been proven over and over.

In any case, Dawkins feels justified in taking a pro-cloning stance mainly because he believes that people who want to clone themselves have the right to do so, and that "the onus is on those who would ban it to spell out what harm it would do, and to whom."

A Right to Clone?

Legislative recommendations proposing the banning of all human cloning sprang into action immediately following the announcement of the birth of Dolly. In the United States, on February 24, 1997, President Bill Clinton asked the recently created National Bioethics Advisory Commission (NBAC) to "undertake a thorough review of the legal and ethical issues associated with the use of this technology." After a series of intensive hearings, the NBAC responded with the recommendation that a ban on human cloning for the purpose of creating a child should be legally instituted.

At the same time, a series of bills making human cloning a federal crime, with penalties as high as a ten-year jail sentence and a $1 million fine, began to be introduced

OPPONENTS OF HUMAN REPRODUCTIVE CLONING MAKE THEIR
FEELINGS KNOWN AT A DEMONSTRATION IN WASHINGTON, D.C.

into Congress. At least a dozen individual states began work on legislative bans on human cloning, as did a number of other countries around the world. In January 1998, 19 European nations signaled their agreement to ban the cloning of human beings, and the United Nations undertook a debate on a treaty to be signed by its 191 member nations, prohibiting human cloning. By the end of 2004, however, the UN failed to reach an agreement on the issue and it put off the debate for another year. Nor, by early 2005, had the U.S. Congress acted on the issue of cloning.

The main reason for the difficulty in arriving at a consensus in the UN, the United States Congress, and elsewhere was the question of whether a ban on human reproductive cloning (cloning to produce babies) should extend to therapeutic cloning (cloning embryonic cells for purposes of medical research and healing).

In therapeutic cloning, embryos would be created so that their cells—known as stem cells—could be used to treat a host of human illnesses. As stem cells were undifferentiated, they could be programmed to grow into almost any kind of body cell, and could be introduced into the body to fight diseases such as cancer, diabetes, Parkinson's disease, and Alzheimer's disease. Stem cell research could also result in cures for paralysis due to spinal cord injuries and perhaps even lead to the growing of replacement organs, with an individual's own DNA. Such organs would not be rejected by the body's immune system because they would be totally compatible with it.

Because of disagreements in legislative bodies as to whether to ban one or both types of human cloning—reproductive and therapeutic—deliberations on anticloning bills in the United States, nationally as well as on the local level in a number of states, were unresolved going into the elections of November 2004. However, with the reelection of President George W. Bush, who opposed both reproductive and therapeutic cloning, it appeared possible that there would be renewed efforts to ban both on the federal level, or at least to influence more states to do so.

There was no such delayed thinking on the part of those who saw human cloning as an opportunity for individuals to exercise their reproductive rights and to demand that they be allowed to do so free from government control. As early as May 25, 1997, *The New York Times Magazine* reported that a Clone Rights United Front had been formed. Under the constitutional guarantees of the right to privacy and the right to liberty it could be argued that there was a right to clone, just as there was a right to make private decisions about the bearing of children. The right to clone was seen as following other rights, such as the freedom to use the newer reproductive technologies of recent decades. These technologies included artificial insemination, in vitro fertilization (IVF), using egg and sperm donors for IVF, and choosing surrogate motherhood, none of which were under government control.

Lee Silver, the Princeton molecular biologist who declared that the birth of Dolly had proved that there were no longer any limits on human reproductive cloning, offered an example of how choosing cloning might be seen as a reasonable extension of IVF. Unable to find an ideal father for the child she would like to have, a woman considers purchasing sperm from "a high-class Internet sperm bank to initiate her pregnancy." She would, however, have to trust the sperm bank to provide her with truthful information about the genetic makeup of the prospective father of her child, and not to conceal any genetic diseases or other negative traits.

Silver's prospective mother realizes that "she doesn't need to mix the genes of some anonymous man with those of her own to bring forth a child. With the new improved nuclear transfer technology, she can do it all by herself."

Like the fictional "Max" in David Rorvik's book, Silver's example can have herself cloned, using in this case one of her body cells and one of her very own eggs, as both donor and recipient cells. Also, she can have the embryo that develops from the transfer implanted into her own uterus, and can carry her own baby to term.

While Silver admitted that his scenario was a bit far-fetched at the time of writing, in 1998, progress made by Korean scientists in embryo cloning that took place six years later, in 2004, brought the possibility of this type of reproductive cloning closer. Silver's scenario also set the stage for a number of other possible ways in which reproductive cloning could be seen as a useful and beneficial technology on a personal and individual level.

Scenarios for Cloning

Human reproductive cloning has been seen, above all, as a new way of dealing with the problem of infertility. Infertile couples who do not want to use an IVF procedure that requires a donated egg or sperm from an unknown individual could have a child who was, at least, a genetic copy of one of them. Theoretically, this could be done by fusing an adult cell from either member of the couple with an enucleated egg. The resulting child would be a carbon copy of the chosen parent.

Of course, unlike offspring who are naturally reproduced, the child would not be a genetic mix of both parents. Would the fact that it bore the genes of only one of them create tension within the family? Or could the problem be balanced somehow by having the next child to be cloned in the family be a product of the other parent's DNA?

Another possible personal benefit of cloning would be the opportunity for a couple to reproduce without the fear of transmitting a known or suspected hereditary disease, such as cystic fibrosis, sickle cell anemia, hemophilia, or a tendency toward emotional or psychiatric problems. Only the genetically healthy parent would be cloned, thus eliminating the threat of producing a child with a hereditary illness.

Gay and lesbian couples might want to choose cloning. In the past, same-sex couples who desired children could not procreate without using donor eggs or sperm from members of the opposite sex. Cloning the DNA of one of the members of a same-sex couple via adult cell nuclear transfer, for example, would offer a genetic copy of at least one member of the couple. In lesbian couples, it would be possible for one of the women to carry the genetic copy to term. Gay couples would, of course, require an enucleated egg and a surrogate mother to bear the offspring of one of the male parents.

There are several other personal reasons for human cloning that advocates of the technology point to as being valid and harming no one. Surely, they say, parents should be allowed the right to "recreate" a beloved family member such as a dying child. Living cells from the child's body could be harvested and frozen. By means of nuclear transfer, the deceased child's DNA could be transferred into an enucleated egg cell, an embryo grown and implanted into the mother's uterus, and a copy of that child brought to term.

In essence the cloned child would be a later twin of the child who died, with an age difference of as many years as took place between the two birth events. However, as in the case of Richard Dawkins's much younger desired clone, there would be differences resulting from changed environmental influences, even if relatively slight ones.

Would knowing that she was a "replacement" child affect the sense of individual identity and personal dignity of the clone? The proclone advocates say no. There have been many cases in which families have sought to replace deceased children with new offspring through natural procreative means. Seeking an exact physical replica through cloning need not stigmatize the child. Rather it would reinforce the sense of being highly prized. On the other hand, naturally procreated "replacement" children might feel the same sense of insufficiency as "replacement" offspring who are clones.

Cloning to Create a Donor

More questionable perhaps than seeking to replace a deceased child with a clone derived from its body cells is the attempt to create a clone to serve as a donor of organs or tissues for a sick family member.

While this is still an unrealized possibility in the world of nuclear cell transfer, in April 1990, a Los Angeles couple deliberately brought into the world an additional offspring for this purpose. Their seventeen-year-old daughter was dying of leukemia and they hoped that the newborn would be a close enough genetic match to supply a bone marrow transplant.

For two years, Mary and Abe Ayala had searched unsuccessfully for a suitable donor for their daughter, Anissa. Although they were told that the chances of producing a sibling who was a match for the older sister were one in four, they took the chance and they met with success.

Medical ethicists, however, were outraged at the idea that parents would purposely create a human being to serve as a source of compatible spare parts for another family member. Seven years later, when the prospect of human cloning appeared on the horizon, cloning advocates pointed to the Ayala case as a perfectly good example of one of the benefits of genetic copying. The Ayalas ran the risk of producing a donor child who was not a match. Only luck was with them. But with nuclear cell transfer, using a body cell from the ailing child, the newborn child was certain to be a genetic copy of the older sibling. Nor, argued those who favored the new technology, was there any reason to believe that the clone would be treated like a spare-parts machine rather than a beloved member of the family.

Louise Brown, who was born as a result of in vitro fertilization in 1978, is known as the world's first "test tube" baby.

Human Cloning Enthusiasts

In 1978, the year in which Louise Brown, the first test-tube baby, was born, James Watson, the co-discoverer of the structure of DNA, was asked by *People* magazine when he thought the first human clone might be created. Watson, who had previously expressed concerns regarding the problems that such a technology might bring about, replied, "Certainly not in any of our lifetimes. I wouldn't be able to predict when we might see the cloning of a mouse, much less a man."

33

Nor did Watson see much point in human cloning, even if the technology were to be developed. "What's to be gained? A carbon copy of yourself?" Watson added that if either of his young sons were to become a scientist, he "would suggest he stay away from cloning. There's no future in it."

The announcement of the birth of Dolly in 1997 dramatically altered Watson's approach to the potential for human cloning. The man whose work with DNA had spurred the development of the science of molecular biology was now an enthusiastic supporter of the genetic revolution. If genetic intervention in the development of plants, animals, and humans was considered "playing God," so be it. Watson's very words, in fact, were, "If we don't play God, who will?"

In an interview with *Scientific American* in April 2003 (the fiftieth anniversary of the DNA discovery), Watson spoke out in favor of freedom of reproductive rights, among other matters. The government, he felt, should stay out of such gene-related issues as genetically engineered foods, abortion, and cloning. "I mean," Watson remarked, "cloning now is the issue. But the first clone is not like the first nuclear bomb going off. It's not going to hurt anyone!"

Watson went on to cite one of the benefits of human cloning—the ability to screen out hereditary diseases by selective genetic copying. True, people might call such offspring "designer babies," but wouldn't it be nice, Watson mused, to be able to say, "My baby's not going to have asthma."

As to being criticized for "playing God," Watson pointed out that change was the very nature of human history. Even the past few hundred years attest to that. "America isn't what it was like when the Pilgrims came here. We've changed everything. We've never tried to respect the past, we've tried to improve on it. And I think any desire to stop people from improving things would be against the human spirit."

An enthusiastic supporter of human cloning from a very different background has been Tom Harkin, a United States senator from the state of Iowa. In response to what he called a "rush to judgment by the Congress of the United States," with regard to introducing bills attempting to ban cloning, Senator Harkin inserted a set of remarks titled "There Are No Appropriate Limits to Human Knowledge" into the Congressional Record on February 9, 1998.

The broad outlines of Senator Harkin's remarks were similar to those of James Watson. He asserted that once science had opened up new avenues of knowledge, and developed accompanying technologies, little could or should be done to stop progress. The central thrust of the senator's argument, however, was that the genetic revolution had enormous potential for good via therapeutic as well as reproductive cloning. Harkin pointed out that if research was allowed to go ahead in the area of genetic transfer technologies utilizing embryonic cells, it might be possible to find cures for a host of serious diseases and afflictions ranging from cancer and diabetes to disabling disorders of the nervous system.

"As long as science is done ethically and openly and with the informed consent of all parties," Harkin wrote, "I do not think Congress should attempt to place limits on the pursuit of knowledge." As to the charge of "playing God," Harkin pointed to the benefits derived so far from once-scorned technologies such as X-rays, IVF, and successful organ transplants. Is human cloning research demeaning to human nature? On the contrary, Harkin stated, "I think that any attempt to limit the pursuit of human knowledge is demeaning to human nature."

What about Clandestine Cloning?

With the birth of Dolly, cloning enthusiasts from the worlds of science and politics attempted to offer valid arguments for the long-range benefits of the new technology to society. But even as James Watson and Tom Harkin were supporting the open pursuit of human knowledge by serious and responsible researchers, a Chicago physicist named Richard Seed made a shattering announcement to the world. In December 1997, Seed, who did not have a medical degree, declared that he would be the first to clone a human being and that the birth would take place within two years.

Seed's stated goal was to offer human cloning as a reproductive answer to infertile couples and to reap from it sufficient glory to win himself a Nobel Prize. He asserted that neither legal restrictions nor ethical reservations would restrain him, threatening to open his human cloning clinic offshore or in a foreign country. Further, Seed defended his position on moral and religious grounds, claiming that God supports cloning. He argued that God would not otherwise have given humans the knowledge of how to clone.

Seed's brash statements and defiant attitude were obviously little more than a publicity stunt. But they raised immediate questions about the hazards of allowing new reproductive technologies to go unregulated by the government. Yet even if the United States managed to pass anticloning laws on the state and/or federal level, what authority could possibly prevail if practitioners such as Seed were to undertake clandestine human cloning operations in an undisclosed or unregulated location outside the country?

Has Human Cloning Already Happened?

Richard Seed, the Chicago physicist who announced in December 1997 that he was about to open a clinic for the cloning of human beings, seemed to fade from the scene shortly afterward, as did an Italian reproductive researcher named Severino Antinori. Antinori had also promised, at the time, that he would soon perform human cloning. A third such figure is Panayiotis Zavos of the Andrology Institute of America in Lexington, Kentucky. On September 15, 2003, Zavos claimed that he would be implanting a human cloned embryo by the end of the year and that a birth would take place in 2004.

Meantime, a group that goes under the name Clonaid, and that keeps its adherents informed of its progress via its Web site, announced that on February 5, 2004, it had produced its sixth cloned human baby. Clonaid's first creation, allegedly born on December 26, 2002, was known as Eve and, like all those who followed her, is said to be normal and healthy in every way. So far, however, reputable scientists who had hoped to do DNA testing on Eve have been frustrated through lack of access.

The founder and driving force behind Clonaid appears to be His Holiness Rael, the spiritual leader of the Raelian Movement, a group that believes in the existence of extraterrestrial beings and UFOs. Rael, a former French sports journalist and race car driver, claims that he is the product of an earthling mother and an extraterrestrial father. In addition to cloning human beings through his company, Clonaid, Rael offers the hope of eternal life once a means is developed for transferring "our memories and personality into our newly cloned brains, which will allow us to truly live forever."

The scientific director of Clonaid is Brigitte Boisselier, a French chemist, who oversees the medical aspects of the

BRIGITTE BOISSELIER, PRESIDENT OF CLONAID, HOLDS A BOOK IN HEBREW SHOWING BABY EVE, ONE OF THE FIVE HUMAN CLONES THE COMPANY CLAIMS TO HAVE CREATED.

company's operation. In October of 2004, Boisselier announced that, as a result of additional pregnancies, a "second generation" of cloned human babies had been born, bringing the total number alive to thirteen. While Clonaid says it has been performing its work at undisclosed locations around the world, it stated that at least one of the cloned babies, although created elsewhere, was born in Australia. Australia has a ban on human reproductive cloning operations.

So far, Clonaid's claims to have produced exact genetic copies of human beings remain unsubstantiated and therefore questionable. But if human reproductive cloning has not already happened, how long will it be before it actually does?

3
Should Human Reproductive Cloning Be Banned?

"Repugnant," "morally despicable," "totally inappropriate," "ethically wrong, socially misguided, and biologically mistaken." These were some of the quotes that appeared in the national media in the weeks immediately following the announcement of Dolly's birth and the possibility that the technology it employed could lead to human reproductive cloning.

The so-called "yuck" factor with regard to cloning human beings was reinforced by a *Time*/CNN poll taken over February 26 and 27, 1997, just after the story broke, in which 90 percent of those questioned said that human cloning should be outlawed.

Supporters might argue for the fundamental human right of freedom of reproduction and for the freedom of science to go in the direction in which it develops. But most anticloning ethicists were deeply concerned with the moral principles at stake, as well as the physical dangers to clones inherent in transferring delicate genetic material from cell to cell. Social thinkers questioned the possible long-term effects of a cloned population on society and even on human evolution. And representatives of many religious groups voiced objections based on the "playing God" aspect of creating clones in soulless laboratories.

The most important issue to those who strongly opposed human cloning on moral grounds was safety. Second, assuming that the hazard could be overcome, what were the possible psychological problems for the clone? How, in the face of personal self-interest and individual agendas on the part of those desiring a clone baby, could the best interests of the clone be protected?

How Safe Would Cloning Be?

In creating Dolly the sheep in 1996, Ian Wilmut and his colleagues fused 277 cells, only 29 of which divided to become embryos. The 29 embryos were implanted in female sheep, only 13 of which became pregnant. Of the 13 pregnant sheep, only one delivered a live birth.

In the years since, success rates with other nonhuman mammals have varied, and it is true that some have been higher. But none have been close to the success rate hoped for in dealing with humans. How much human risk in creating clones would individuals and society be prepared to accept? Unsuccessful experiments with sheep generally have been considered acceptable except by animal rights advocates. But unsuccessful experiments with human beings would entail huge costs in terms of psychological and physical damage, and scientists and their backers who undertook the cloning of humans could be sued for enormous sums of money if things went wrong.

What are some of the things that could go wrong? In conventional reproduction, through the fusing of the sperm and the egg, the presence of an extra Chromosome 21 is known to produce a Down syndrome child. Such children suffer from abnormalities in their appearance and are mentally impaired to varying degrees. In nuclear transfer technology, there is a reasonably broad possibility that chromosomes will not replicate normally, resulting in a variety of developmental problems while still in the uterus and leading ultimately to miscarriage. But developing organisms with such chromosomal abnormalities do not always die. The clone baby could then be born with serious defects and disabilities, perhaps even of a monstrous variety not yet seen in nature.

Or a clone baby could appear to be perfectly normal at birth but, as in the case of Dolly, might soon begin to reflect the age of the adult cell from which its genetic material was taken. Dolly died young, quite possibly because her donor parent was a six-year-old sheep who had already lived half her life span, making Dolly perhaps seven years old when her chronological age was only one. What aging effects might show up prematurely in a human clone child who had been created from the skin cell, for example, of a thirty-, forty-, or even fifty-year-old donor parent?

Arthur L. Caplan, director of the Center for Bioethics of the University of Pennsylvania Health System, feels that the safety risk is so great that "to create a human clone based on the existing success record of animal cloning would be blatantly immoral. The clone could be born deformed, dying, or prematurely aging. There would be no basis for taking such a risk unless there were some overwhelmingly powerful reason to clone someone. . . . At what point will enough data from animals be on hand to justify a human trial?. . . Who should attempt to clone and for what reasons?"

Safety, then, is first among the concerns that are likely to lead to a ban on human reproductive cloning. Safety cannot be guaranteed by even the most enthusiastic and scientifically sophisticated of procloning advocates. Assuming, however, that cloning humans with minimal risk will one day become a possibility, what are the other moral objections to putting the technology into practice?

Some Psychological Hazards of Being a Clone

Does a clone have an individual identity? What burdens might a clone have to bear, in terms of its physical resemblance to a parent or other family member who donated the genetic material that made it? What expectations would the donor have of the clone? Suppose the clone was created not only to resemble but to achieve the capabilities of a demanding parent desiring an heir, or was created in the genetic image of a major figure in the world of sports, entertainment, intellectual greatness, or musical genius? And what about the biological destiny of a clone designed to be a blood, tissue, or organ donor for its creator?

Defenders of human reproductive cloning do not see mere physical resemblance as a challenge to psychological well-being in terms of individuality and personal identity. They point out that in the United States about one in every four hundred births are identical twins, which are genetically even more alike than nuclear transfer clones. (Identical twins result from the splitting of a fertilized egg, while in nuclear transfer tiny organs in a cell that have their own DNA and are known as mitochondria are retained in small amounts in the enucleated egg.) Yet the overwhelming majority of twins do not appear to suffer from serious psychological problems resulting from physical likeness.

Clones, in fact, may be viewed simply as later-born twins, who will have the opportunity to be even more differentiated because of environmental variations during their period of gestation and the circumstances of the time and place into which they are born.

Anticloning ethicists, however, feel that the motivation for cloning is often based on selfishness and narcissism—more often than in the case of children produced by traditional reproductive means. Leon Kass, a bioethicist at the

EVEN IF IT WERE POSSIBLE TO CLONE THE EIGHTEENTH-CENTURY MUSICAL GENIUS, MOZART, WHO IS PICTURED WRITING MUSIC IN THIS ENGRAVING, HIS TALENT WOULD BE MOST UNLIKELY TO BLOSSOM IN A SIMILAR WAY TODAY.

Cloning Another Sports Hero, Another Mozart

Cloning for the purpose of duplicating human beings with great talent in the fields of sports or entertainment, or of replicating musical or scientific geniuses, is tempting as an argument for both enhancing our personal lives and enriching society at large.

We are told, however, that such fantasies are unlikely to materialize, even in environments that favor their development. The cloned offspring of a great basketball player, for example, might be so pressured by the expectations of his genetic donor parent that he would withdraw from the scene and turn his efforts in a completely different direction.

As to other types of greatness, could the musical genius of a Mozart be passed on through cloning, assuming that some of his adult cells had been culled and frozen for future use prior to his death in 1791? Here, we immediately encounter the problems of environmental differences between Mozart's day and today. Mozart's inventiveness and the variety of his work were influenced by his father's musical input, by the atmosphere of eighteenth-century Europe, and by the demands for musical works by his royal and wealthy patrons.

A Mozart clone born in the twenty-first century would have no direct exposure to the world in which his genetic donor lived. His musical side might develop into that of a rock musician or a rap artist. The historical Mozart was also playful and a jokester, so the musical side of him might have been entirely suppressed and he might have turned out to be a stand-up comedian. Once more, the question of nurture versus nature comes into play.

University of Chicago, writes, "Cloning is inherently despotic, for it seeks to make one's children (or someone else's children) after one's own image (or an image of one's choosing) and their future according to one's will. In some cases, the despotism may be mild and benevolent. In other cases it will be mischievous and downright tyrannical. But despotism—the control of another through one's will—it inevitably will be."

While this anticloning view may appear extreme, it is true that the cloned child is robbed of the right to be genetically unique because its conception was not the result of a sexual mating in which random hereditary factors are allowed to operate freely. In terms of preserving human dignity, it may be unfair to create a child who knows she is the identical twin of one parent or of some other beloved or esteemed individual to whom he or she is constantly being compared. Also, what are the interfamily relationships in cases where a child has been cloned from one of its parents? The mother of a cloned female child, for example, is also its sister. Are the child's mother's/sister's biological parents its parents or its grandparents? Confusion over lineage, kinship ties, and family-member identity might develop all too easily in trying to sort out relationships in the clone family tree.

Lastly, as already discussed among psychological hazards for the clone, is the possibility that an individual with the same DNA would be created for the purpose of serving as a source of compatible organs and tissues for its genetic donor. The clone could be called upon to donate, for example, blood (especially if a rare type), skin for grafts, bone marrow, and a spare organ such as a kidney in order to cure or prolong the life of the person from whom it was cloned.

While such sacrifices might not be physically harmful to the clone, aside from the medical and surgical procedures involved, anticloning ethicists see the possibility of serious psychological effects. Also, without any sort of legal restriction against creating clones to serve as sources of spare parts for other humans, how far might this practice be taken? The deliberate and dehumanizing creation of a subordinate class of individuals to be plundered for their parts becomes the stuff of nightmares. On the other hand, it is entirely possible that a cloned human would not only be happy to be alive but proud to be able to donate tissues and even organs to save another human life.

Possible Effects of Human Cloning on Society

What are the prospects for the human species in a society where reproductive cloning is unfettered and freely practiced? Who, first of all, will undertake cloning on the broadest scale and for what purpose? The answer, say anticloning social thinkers, will be the rich and the powerful, and their purposes will vary depending on their specific desires or needs.

In the most frightening scenarios, despotic rulers could use human cloning to create armies to serve as cannon fodder for their rogue regimes. Similarly, such dictators, patterned after Adolf Hitler, could also create a slave society to serve on the home front during their campaigns of foreign aggression.

While the foregoing example of how governments might use cloning may appear extreme, it does seem plausible that wealthy individuals will be the ones to pay the high cost of creating genetic copies of themselves, and that the result of their doing so will be an elitist society. Cloned offspring, chosen to replicate the best physical and mental characteristics in the families of the wealthy, might well become the ruling class of the future. All the rest of society—those individuals born in the natural way through the union of sperm and egg—might make up the great underclass.

Is Cloning the New Eugenics?

The government-implemented eugenics movement in the United States took root in the late 1800s, a period of high rates of immigration from eastern and southern Europe, whose inhabitants were considered less desirable than those from northern Europe. Other "undesirables" at the time were immigrants from China and Japan, as well as the native African-American population that had been slaves until the Civil War.

Instances of pauperism, criminality, prostitution, and unscientific assessments of mental retardation among these less favored members of American society were ascribed to hereditary, or genetic, defects. As a result, between 1907 and 1931, thirty states adopted eugenics laws to "breed out" such unwanted traits as feeblemindedness, insanity, criminal tendencies, and epilepsy, through the sterilization of males and females of childbearing age.

Although it was obvious that the states' eugenics laws were being used as instruments of racism, ethnic prejudice, and antifeminism, the United States Supreme Court upheld the compulsory sterilization of the "unfit." Writing for the Court majority in 1927, Justice Oliver Wendell Holmes declared, "Three generations of imbeciles are enough."

It was only with the advent of Nazism in Hitler's Germany in 1933 that the support for "improving" the population by "breeding out" certain undesirables began to fade in the United States. Most Americans were horrified to learn of the Nazi undertaking to create a "pure Aryan race" of blond, blue-eyed, Nordic types by annihilating Jews, Gypsies, Slavic peoples, and other non-Aryans, as well as Germans who were deformed, crippled, or mentally ill.

The purpose of the eugenics movement of the twentieth century was to create more perfect individuals by eliminating so-called negative genetic traits. The eugenics of the twenty-first century seeks the opposite—the improvement of humankind by breeding in or genetically implanting positive traits. Supporters of human reproductive cloning oppose government intervention regarding the use of the new technology, and point to the evils of the compulsory sterilization of the feebleminded in the bad old days in the United States.

On the other hand, those who favor a ban on the production of designer babies point to the dangers of a future society of superhumans who will hold sway over a vast underclass, and they strongly support the introduction of legislation to prevent the new technology from running rampant.

In his book *Remaking Eden: Cloning and Beyond in a Brave New World* Princeton biologist Lee Silver sees both human reproductive cloning and germline engineering (the modification of embryos in their earliest stages through the insertion of selected human genes) as the ultimate means of improving humankind.

The manipulation of human genes is still in its infancy, and early experiments with their insertion in the human body to combat disease—through what is known as gene therapy—have been perilous. But Silver is unapologetic in his belief in the value of cloning and human genetic engineering as a way of creating mentally and physically superior individuals, even if it means dividing society into two distinct classes.

In his scenario for the year 2350, Silver compares what he calls the GenRich (genetically enriched members of society) with the Naturals (neither clones nor germline engineered humans). In time, Silver tells us, "the GenRich class and the Natural class will become . . . entirely separate species with no ability to cross-breed, and with as much romantic interest in each other as a current human would have for a chimpanzee."

To those concerned with the future of society in a world where human selection through reproductive cloning and other forms of genetic management are freely practiced, the new technology of the early twenty-first century begins to bear an eerie resemblance to the discredited eugenics movement of the early twentieth century. In the early 1900s, eugenics concerned itself with breeding humans to exclude certain undesirable traits. Today, the genetic modification of humans to breed for the inclusion of certain desirable traits appears to be another form of eugenics.

Another long-range effect of human reproductive cloning on society, as seen by concerned social thinkers, is the possibility that it would limit the biodiversity of the human race. As is already evident in the plant and animal world, genetic engineering for the purpose of producing a superior, if not perfect, banana, potato, ear of corn, soybean, or milk cow, has resulted in the loss of many varieties of those species that once existed. Limited diversity within a species means that, by virtue of sharing a common DNA—and thus a common immune system—organisms have limited defenses against germs, viruses, parasites, insects, and other harmful effects of nature.

As natural history tells us, it is only through variety that a species can maintain its defenses against environmental change. In the human species, it is sexual reproduction that produces the novel combinations of genes that provide the resources to respond to the ongoing challenges of nature.

Supporters of human reproductive cloning, however, respond with the argument that it is not likely that there would be millions of clones of one individual, all bearing the same DNA, in any given part of the world. Therefore, it is doubtful that large human populations would be wiped out by an epidemic or other threat of nature because they belonged to a human gene pool that lacked an immune response to that specific threat.

On the other hand, it's possible that families of wide-ranging groups of cloned individuals might be subject to tragic and unforeseen diseases or deaths as a result of inbreeding via their shared DNA. Ironically, the search for human perfection through genetic selection could be the very stuff of human demise.

Some Religious Views of Human Reproductive Cloning

"Cloning risks being the tragic parody of God's omnipotence." These were the words of Pope John Paul II in 1997, on the occasion of the first discussions about human reproductive cloning, following the announcement of the

POPE JOHN PAUL II, SEEN HERE WITH PRESIDENT GEORGE W. BUSH IN 2001, READS A STATEMENT OPPOSING BOTH REPRODUCTIVE CLONING AND STEM CELL RESEARCH. THE POPE DIED IN THE SPRING OF 2005, BUT THE POLICIES OF THE ROMAN CATHOLIC CHURCH DID NOT CHANGE.

birth of Dolly the sheep via somatic-cell nuclear transfer technology.

Pope John Paul II, who did not testify publicly, was expressing the view taken by most of the religious leaders who did testify before the National Bioethics Advisory Commission (NBAC), which was called into session by U.S. President Bill Clinton that year. Although Catholic, Protestant, Jewish, and Islamic positions in opposition to cloning varied somewhat, all appeared to agree that it was a form of playing God that ran counter to the tenets of their religion.

Judeo-Christians pointed out that the Bible describes humans as created "in the image of God" (Genesis 1:27). If humankind is created in God's likeness, should it be created by human manipulation? Wouldn't imitation of the creative power of God be a sin of pride? In addition, most religious views emphasized the preservation of the family and the procreation of children within a committed marital relationship. They cited God's command to male and female to "be fruitful and multiply" (Genesis 1:28) as evidence that cloning would be a transgression against the creator and an encroachment on the creator's domain. As a result, many theologians feared it would be questionable whether a clone would have a soul.

Roughly one-quarter of those testifying before the NBAC represented religious groups. Southern Baptists and other fundamentalist Protestant sects were as strong as the Roman Catholic contingent in asking for an immediate ban on human reproductive cloning. Muslim leaders, too, pressed for a ban. They viewed the human body as a trust from God. Munawar Ahmad Anees, editor-in-chief of *Periodica Islamica*, wrote, "The arrogance of Western science has never been greater than when it crossed the boundary of cloning. . . . Is it the vengeful self-perpetuation of those who would defy God? . . . The human body is God's property, not man's laboratory."

"STORM TROOPER" CLONES ENACT AN ATTACK AS PART OF A FRIGHTENING SCENARIO FOR THE CHARITY PREMIERE OF A *STAR WARS* MOVIE AT A HOLLYWOOD THEATER.

There were, however, other views. Some Jewish rabbis representing less orthodox branches of the religion did not see the creation story in Genesis as calling for a total ban on human cloning. Buddhist views, too, were tolerant of cloning for the most part because of their belief that there is no such thing as two identical existent beings despite their genetic makeup. Each individual is separate, and nothing can be duplicated in a nonrepeatable universe. The Buddhist concern was mainly that the motivation behind the cloning should be for the benefit of others.

If cloning is against God's will in the view of so many theologians, what scientific developments are permissible and in keeping with God's will? Is it acceptable to treat the sick with proven medicines and surgical procedures? Should anesthesia be employed to alleviate pain? Should autopsies be performed to determine the cause of death and instruct us how to better treat human ills and medical emergencies? These were the questions that still other religious leaders were asking as a result of the NBAC consensus that a federal legislative ban should be imposed on human reproductive cloning.

Although no such legislation had yet been enacted by 2004, President George W. Bush reiterated a vow made earlier during his administration to ban both stem cell research (cloning embryonic cells for therapeutic purposes) and human reproductive cloning. Speaking to the National Association of Evangelicals (Protestants who read the Bible as the word of God and have a commitment to winning converts to their religious faith) in Colorado Springs, Colorado, on March 11, 2004, Bush made the following remarks: "I oppose the use of federal funds for the destruction of embryos for stem cell research and I will work with Congress to pass a comprehensive and effective ban on human cloning. Human life is a creation of God, not a commodity to be exploited by man."

4

Should We Clone Human Cells to Cure Illnesses?

The years immediately following the 1997 announcement of Dolly's birth witnessed a storm of ethical, moral, social, and religious debates concerning the issue of human reproductive cloning via somatic-cell nuclear transfer. By the early 2000s, however, even the most enthusiastic supporters of creating clone babies appeared to have come around to the view that duplicating people did not have a very high priority as one of the developments growing out of the genetic revolution.

Lee Silver, the Princeton molecular biologist who projected a world of "GenRich versus Natural" humans in his 1997 book, *Remaking Eden*, stated in 2004 that while he still thought human cloning was "going to happen . . . I'm not saying it's good."

Other scientists, who had once seen reproductive cloning as the direction in which modern genetics was taking society, had already put that technology on the back burner in favor of the much more promising development of therapeutic cloning.

Technically, both reproductive cloning and therapeutic cloning begin in much the same way in the laboratory. A human egg cell is stripped of its nucleus, which contains its genetic material. An adult cell with a full genetic code is fused with the enucleated egg. The injected egg is then stimulated either by an electric pulse or a mixture of chemicals to activate it so that it begins to divide into additional cells.

The object of both reproductive and therapeutic nuclear cell transfer is the same—to create a human embryo, the cluster of cells that represents the earliest stages of growth. But the use to which the embryo would be put is different. In human reproductive cloning, an embryo that had reached the blastocyst stage (100 to 150 embryonic cells, consisting of a hard outer covering enclosing a mass of inner cells) could theoretically be implanted in a human uterus, where it would attach itself to the uterine wall. The embryo would proceed to grow into a fetus (the next stage of development) and finally into a fully developed infant.

In therapeutic cloning, implantation for reproduction would not take place. At the blastocyst stage, the embryo contains the valuable stem cells that are still what is known as totipotent, or pluripotent—undifferentiated, as opposed to more developed cells—and therefore theoretically capable of being developed into any of the body's tissues and organs.

How Stem Cells Would Work in Therapeutic Cloning

Stem cells derived via nuclear transfer technology from the person who contributed the adult cell to make the embryo would be genetically identical to that person. The next step would be to learn how to direct the stem cells to become brain cells to treat diseases such as Parkinson's and Alzheimer's, or nerve cells to repair damaged spinal cords that have inflicted a permanent state of paralysis. Or, through their ability to differentiate, stem cells could be directed to develop into pancreatic cells to treat diabetes, or into bone marrow, skin, or other human tissues. Even further in the direction of healing the body through stem-cell research and development lies the possibility of growing entire organs such as kidneys or a liver or pancreas to replace damaged or failing body parts.

The obvious advantage of harvesting stem cells from embryos cloned from our own body cells is that the new tissues and/or organs would consist of our own DNA and hence would be totally compatible. There would be no danger that our transplanted tissues or remade body parts would be rejected by our immune systems.

Reduced to its simplest terms, the procedure for creating stem cells with our own DNA in order to treat, for example, a form of leukemia (a condition in which there are too many white cells in the blood due to faulty manufacture in the bone marrow) would be as follows. We grow our own healthy replacement bone marrow by fusing the genetic material from one of our adult body cells with that of an enucleated donor egg. The fused egg is allowed to divide a few times to develop embryonic cells, or stem cells, which have the potential to develop into any kind of body cell.

These stem cells are directed to become bone marrow cells by a laboratory process and are then introduced into the body as a bone marrow transplant. What started out to be a clone of the adult-cell donor has become a means of therapy to heal a specific life-threatening disease in that person. Nor is there any danger that the body's immune system will reject the bone marrow transplant because it consists of that individual's DNA and is therefore genetically identical bone marrow.

The use of stem-cell therapy as practiced on humans is still in its very early stages. Experiments done on animals, however, have shown remarkably hopeful results. Rats that had been paralyzed as a result of spinal cord injuries, and that received transplants of nerve cells derived from human embryonic stem cells, were able to walk again. This experiment was conducted by a private biotechnology company researching stem cell therapy—Geron Corporation of Menlo Park, California—and the finding was reported on July 3, 2003, in *New Scientist* magazine.

Geron warned, however, that the first trials with human patients would probably be successful only with those individuals who had suffered recent spinal cord injuries. Patients who had been paralyzed for many years or who had degenerative nerve diseases probably would be difficult to treat.

Another private company, Advanced Cell Technology (ACT), of Worcester, Massachusetts, reported success treating damaged mouse hearts with stem cells. *The New Zealand Herald* reported on February 12, 2004, that according to ACT, "stem cells taken from cloned mice were able to regenerate mouse hearts damaged by heart attacks by forming tiny blood vessels and heart muscle cells." Work with human patients, however, to attempt to repair diseased hearts by infusing stem cells is still in its infancy.

Milestones in Stem Cell Research

It is doubtful that most people, other than those scientists involved in animal cloning and other aspects of the genetic revolution, had even heard of stem cells until 1998. In that year the biologist James Thomson, working with a group

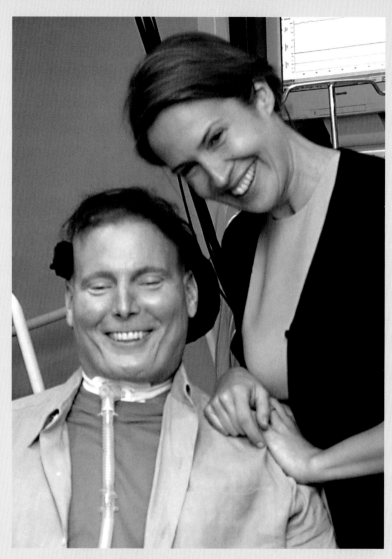

ACTOR CHRISTOPHER REEVE, FAMOUS FOR HIS PORTRAYAL OF SUPERMAN IN SEVERAL MOVIES, SMILES WITH HIS WIFE AT THE BUTLER LABORATORY AT THE PRINCE OF WALES MEDICAL RESEARCH INSTITUTE IN SYDNEY, AUSTRALIA IN 2003. REEVE, WHO WAS PARALYZED FROM THE NECK DOWN AS A RESULT OF A RIDING ACCIDENT IN 1996, WAS AN OUTSPOKEN ADVOCATE OF THERAPEUTIC CLONING UNTIL HIS DEATH IN OCTOBER 2004.

The Case of Christopher Reeve

In 1995 the actor Christopher Reeve, known for having played Superman in the movies and for many other roles both on the stage and in film, suffered a severe horseback-riding accident that damaged his spinal cord and left him paralyzed from the shoulders down.

Reeve, who used a wheelchair until his death in October 2004 due to the longterm effects of paralysis, was an outspoken advocate of stem-cell research. He saw it as being a strong potential source of nerve cell repair for individuals who, like himself, had lost the ability to walk, as well as many other functions, through damage to the spinal cord as a result of a badly fractured spinal column. The work done at Geron Corporation with paralyzed rats was of special interest to Reeve. Researchers there have developed a means of transforming embryonic stem cells into specialized glial cells, which nurture the nerves of the spinal cord and have the potential to reactivate them.

Reeve was impatient with those researchers who believed that they needed to test on animals for years before administering therapies to humans. He felt that the application of stem cell therapies to human patients was too slow, even though it involved risk. "Because," Reeve stated, "let's face it, nothing of any significance has ever been achieved without reasonable risk." Meanwhile, the wheelchair-bound actor and activist pointed to examples of patients similar to himself in places like China and Israel who had been treated with stem cell therapy and had experienced varying degrees of improvement. He also railed against the limited number of stem cell lines—colonies derived from a single embryo—that were approved for research via federal funding by President Bush in August 2001. Because limiting sources of embryonic stem cells limits research, Reeve said, "We are rapidly falling behind other countries."

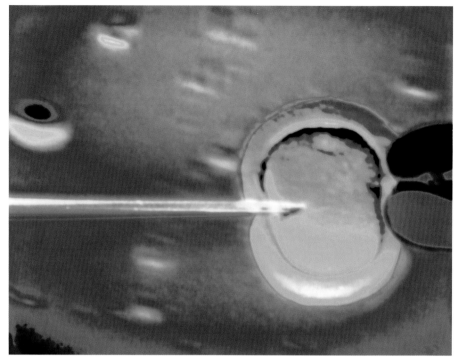

IN VITRO FERTILIZATION HAS BEEN USED SINCE THE 1970S TO AID HUMAN REPRODUCTION. THOUGH HUMANS ARE NOT CLONED THROUGH THIS METHOD, PEOPLE WHO WOULD NOT OTHERWISE EXIST ARE BORN THIS WAY.

at the University of Wisconsin, announced that he had isolated stem cells from human embryos and grown them, through laboratory culture, into five cell lines. The embryos were derived from fertilized human eggs—the result of sperm and egg fusion outside the uterus—attained through in vitro fertilization.

As the IVF process often produces more embryos than are needed for implantation to create a test-tube baby, the additional embryos may be frozen for possible future use. Such embryos may also be donated to science, with the consent of the couples who have undergone IVF, for use as the source of privately funded stem cell lines.

While stem cells derived from donated IVF embryos provide an excellent means of researching the potential of stem cells to mature into many different cell types, they do not have the advantage of being genetically identical to the individual requiring stem cell therapy. So, in 2001, biotechnologists at the Worcester, Massachusetts, company Advanced Cell Technology attempted to develop a human embryo from the fusion of a human egg and an adult body cell via nuclear transfer technology, and to derive stem cells from it.

Twelve female volunteers (later reduced to seven) were chosen to contribute the donor eggs. The women, whose health was carefully screened, agreed to take the necessary hormone injections to increase ovulation, or human egg production. Among the adult body cells used, some were taken from individuals who were likely to benefit from therapeutic cloning because they suffered from diabetes or had a spinal cord injury.

Although several methods for producing a blastocyst—an embryonic stage consisting of 100 to 150 cells, including the valuable stem cells—were attempted, Advanced Cell Technology did not succeed in getting any of the embryos to progress beyond the six-cell stage. The effort to produce stem cells with a designated genetic identity had failed.

In 2003, Advanced Cell Technology tried again to replace the DNA in human eggs with the DNA in human body cells in order to facilitate a means of therapeutic cloning. This time, the biotechnology company was able to develop a human embryo that reached the sixteen-cell stage, known as a morula, which precedes the blastula stage. Success, however, in obtaining stem cells remained out of reach.

Therapeutic cloning experts elsewhere in the world were also working at the time on the creation of human

THE SOUTH KOREAN STEM-CELL RESEARCHER DR. WOO SUK HWANG IS SEEN TESTING A COW'S EGG FOR MAD COW DISEASE, WHICH HAS CAUSED FATALITIES IN HUMANS.

embryos for the extraction of stem cells. In February 2004, two South Korean scientists announced that, following the lines of the researchers at Advanced Cell Technology, they had met with unprecedented success.

Woo Suk Hwang, a researcher in animal cloning, and Shin Yong Moon, M.D., of Seoul National University, led the work. They began by choosing sixteen female volunteers from whom they obtained 242 donated eggs. The large number of donated eggs made it possible for the researchers to experiment with various means of producing blastocysts that would not only yield stem cells but would produce cells that could be cultured in the laboratory to grow into long-lived stem cell lines, or colonies.

The work of the South Korean scientists was significant because they "ended up with 30 blastocysts, from which they were able to extract 20 inner cell masses." Also, they were able to grow one of the cell masses into a stem cell line. While the cell line success rate could be viewed as only one out of 242, the scientific community hailed the news. It was seen as an important technical advance and a recipe for further development in the production of the valuable undifferentiated stem cells that had so much potential for curing human diseases and disabilities.

The Debate about Therapeutic Cloning

The landmark achievement of Hwang and Moon, cloning human cells to produce embryos, revived the debate about cloning in general that had been going on since the announcement of Dolly's birth. The South Korean scientists had made it clear from the start that they had no intention of implanting the embryos they produced in humans for purposes of reproduction. But those who opposed human reproductive cloning contended that the techniques used by the South Korean researchers would make it easier for someone somewhere to create a clone baby.

In addition, many arguments against the South Korean research arose from the contention that growing a human embryo with the potential of becoming a human being if implanted in a uterus and then destroying it to harvest the stem cells was a form of murder. Once again, the issue of cloning, even solely for purposes of research and medical therapy, gave rise to intense discussion.

A leading opponent of cloning, Leon Kass of the University of Chicago, was also the chairman of President George W. Bush's Council on Bioethics at the time of the South Korean announcement. Kass called for immediate federal legislation to place a ban on all human cloning, whether therapeutic or reproductive. "Today," he warned, "cloned blastocysts for research, tomorrow cloned blastocysts for babymaking."

Pro-life groups weighed in with the view that therapeutic cloning created life only to destroy it, and that harvesting stem cells from embryos was a form of discrimination against the most vulnerable and helpless form of life. Some religious leaders, however, who strongly opposed reproductive cloning, were not as against the issue of therapeutic cloning. Representatives of many Jewish groups tended to be more accepting of therapeutic cloning because of the belief that there is a moral and ethical command to heal the human body.

Advocates of therapeutic cloning asserted that embryos that are given life in the laboratory are different from those that are conceived through the joining of egg and sperm. Such blastocysts would never be found in nature and should not be thought of as human life if the intention is that they be used for healing only. Taken to extremes, one could say that, with laboratory manipulation, any cell in the human body could be the beginning of a new person.

Also in favor of embryonic stem cell research for therapeutic cloning were those members of the scientific community who see the United States falling behind other nations because of the very limited federal research funding and the potential for a federal ban on further research. On August 9, 2001, President Bush officially declared that only the sixty existing stem cell lines would be available for federally funded research and that no further lines would be created. By February 2004, only fifteen stem cell lines remained available to institutions seeking government grants for stem cell research, and Bush's reelection in November 2004 was a further blow to the possibility of federal funding.

Also, opponents of stem cell research clung to the view that therapeutic cloning was a slippery slope that was all too likely to lead to reproductive cloning, possibly on a major scale. Yet other opponents joined them, warning that the technology was, in itself, fraught with hazards.

So far scientists have learned to manipulate only some of the undifferentiated embryonic cells into specialized cells, and there is much more work to be done to expand their application. Nor can human trials begin before the experiments done on animals are validated and replicated.

In a report in *The New York Times* on the occasion of the South Korean announcement, Steven A. Goldman, M.D., chief of the division of cell and gene therapy at the University of Rochester Medical Center, cautioned that "cell populations to be implanted must be pure." There are so-called residual embryonic stem cells that "tend to form tumors called teratomas that consist of a mix of tissue types including hair, skin, and teeth."

Goldman also stated that "for treating certain neurologic diseases, implanting the wrong type of nerve cell could cause side effects like seizures."

Adult Stem Cells versus Embryonic Stem Cells

With fierce moral, ethical, and religious arguments raging over the creation of embryos for the harvesting of stem cells, researchers have turned to investigating other sources of stem cells.

Primitive, or undifferentiated, cells that may serve as medical therapies for a variety of human ills are found in such waste products as the placenta and the umbilical cord. The placenta is the blood-filled organ that unites the fetus and the uterus up to the time of birth. The umbilical cord is the ropelike tissue connecting the fetus with the placenta.

Additional sources of stem cells found in the bodies of adults are the brain, the bone marrow, and the nose. All of

Can Nasal Stem Cells Repair Spinal Injuries?

In April 2004, it was reported that a series of remarkable experiments in the repair of spinal cord injuries was being carried out at the Hospital de Egas Moniz, a large public hospital in Lisbon, Portugal. Young American and European patients who had recently suffered paralysis as a result of accidents that injured their spinal cords underwent surgery for regenerative medicine under the supervision of Carlos Lima, M.D., the hospital's chief of neuropathology.

Lima's approach was to extract adult stem cells from the patient's nose and to transplant them around the damaged spinal nerve tissue in a single surgical procedure. The nasal stem cells were not manipulated to become nerve cells. The hope was that these as yet undifferentiated cells would wrap themselves around the nerve fiber and regenerate it. It is believed that such transplanted adult cells, packed around the spinal cord, will remain active for months, or even years, making for continued improvement in the patient's condition.

Using the patient's own body cells guarantees that there will be no rejection of the transplanted tissue. But intensive and ongoing physical therapy is absolutely essential, according to Lima, if the paralysis is to be overcome. Although there have been no complete recoveries so far, results have been encouraging, with patients reporting varying degrees of restored movement and sensation in the afflicted parts of the body.

these organs and tissues keep on producing localized stem cells for the purpose of replenishing lost cells throughout the life of an adult. The cells start out as primitive cells but soon become differentiated, depending on their destiny.

If the cells can be procured from the adult body while they are still in an early stage of development, they may be manipulated in the laboratory to become specialized cells, such as nerve cells. Or they may be used without manipulation and simply implanted in the body in the hope that they will take their developmental signal from the tissue to which they are bonded, and generate healthy new cells. The direct implantation of adult stem cells into the human body's trouble spots is in the early stages of experimentation, and has been practiced so far on a very limited scale.

In addition to using nasal stem cells to treat spinal cord injuries, other therapies with adult stem cells have been tried. They include the repair of damaged heart tissue with stem cells harvested from the patient's own bone marrow. A child with lymphoma also was successfully treated with a transplant of umbilical-cord blood from an infant brother who was a perfect genetic match. The chance of finding such a match among non-clone siblings is one in four.

Looking farther into the future, some researchers see adult stem cells as a means not only of harnessing the body's own ability to heal itself but as a way of slowing the very phenomenon of human aging. Meanwhile the controversy and concerns regarding stem cell research—particularly the production of embryos from cloned cells—and its potential application for therapeutic or even the much contested reproductive cloning process goes on.

5

Should We Try to Genetically Engineer Humans?

What is genetic engineering and how does it relate to cloning? Mice were the first among the animals to be genetically engineered for purposes of biomedical research. Among large animals, such as cows, pigs, and sheep, genetic engineering has been going on since the 1980s, as we learned in looking at the story behind the birth of Dolly.

To create the farm animals that could become "living drug factories," for example, the scientists at the Roslin Institute introduced into sheep the human gene for the blood-clotting protein to treat hemophiliacs. This process of gene transfer, or transgenic modification (the transfer of a gene from one species into another), resulted in the animal's delivery of milk from which the clotting-factor drug could be extracted and then used to treat hemophilia in humans.

Once the cells were modified, cloning was employed to make exact copies of the genetically modified animals, for that was the only way to ensure that a line of offspring with the same DNA and thus the same therapeutic features could be developed.

As we search for more effective ways to treat diseases

and disabilities in humans, is it feasible to apply the process of genetic engineering by implanting healthy genes to replace defective ones? Or, taking the process even further, could we also alter or even remove undesirable genes? In humans, genetic or germline engineering would most likely involve the use of human genes only. But it is also possible that it might involve the transfer of genes from one species to another as in the genetic modification of animals.

The prospect of cloning humans by nuclear cell transfer for purposes of reproduction appears to have drawn closer because of successful work with animals, specifically Dolly. Even though there is ongoing controversy with regard to the safety of human reproductive cloning and to the moral, ethical, and religious principles at stake, its achievement is technically within reach.

The manipulation of human genes, however, either for purposes of medical therapy or to create a super race of genetically enhanced "designer" humans, appears to be a more distant promise. Clinical trials to cure certain diseases with gene therapy (a procedure that does not affect the germline, but treats only the diseased individual) began in 1990, after first being tested on mice, rhesus monkeys, and baboons. But the highly publicized death of an eighteen-year-old volunteer in a gene therapy experiment in the United States in 1999 created serious doubts as to whether the procedure was ready for human trial. Three years later, in 2002, a gene therapy trial in France was halted when one of the children being treated for a severe immune deficiency syndrome known as the "bubble boy" disease developed leukemia.

The Human Genome Project

Finding out about genetic mutations and how they could cause diseases and disorders of many kinds resulted directly from the discovery of the structure of human DNA

A Gene Therapy Experiment and the Death of Jesse Gelsinger

Jesse Gelsinger, eighteen, was born with a rare metabolic disorder that caused an excessive amount of ammonia to accumulate in his blood. His disease was caused by a genetic mutation, probably inherited from his mother, as women are generally carriers of the disease. While a high ammonia level in the blood can cause coma and even death, Jesse was able to control his condition with diet and drugs. The young Arizona resident was not sick or in medical danger when he signed up for an experiment at the University of Pennsylvania to investigate the safety of a treatment for babies who were born with a fatal form of the same disease that Jesse had.

The purpose of the experiment was to cure the mutation-caused disease by replacing the defective gene with a healthy one. But the method for delivering the dose of corrective genes into Jesse's cells involved the use of a weakened cold virus. The virus served as a vector, or carrier, because it had the ability to get inside the cells and make changes in them. Tests on animals and on one human patient at the University of Pennsylvania had shown that the virus caused some mild flu-like side effects and some mild inflammation of the liver. But in Jesse's case, the virus appeared to have triggered such a severe reaction that he suffered liver, kidney, and lung failure—a multiple organ breakdown.

On September 17, 1999, four days after his gene therapy treatment began, Jesse Gelsinger died. Although other patients in the clinical trial group survived, most had received lower doses of the virus or had received the same dosage but from a different lot. Jesse's death might have been caused by the virus used to carry the gene infusion, by a severe immune system response, or by human error. In any case, it raised a red flag with regard to the safety of gene therapies as an effective treatment for genetic disease.

Another problem that has made gene therapy questionable is that it may be only a short-lived cure for the disease at hand. Due to the rapidly dividing nature of cells, the therapeutic DNA introduced into the cells may not remain stable and functional. As a result, the patient might have to undergo successive rounds of gene therapy.

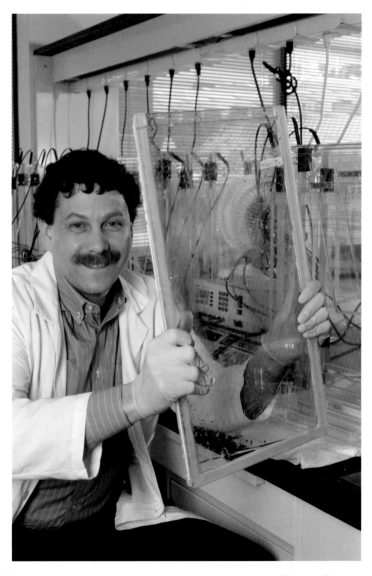

ONE OF THE MANY RESEARCHERS PARTICIPATING IN THE HUMAN GENOME PROJECT HOLDS A GEL PLATE USED FOR SEQUENCING THE GENES OF MICE.

by James Watson and Francis Crick in 1953. By the 1970s, scientists could already isolate certain genes and detect mistakes in the genetic code that were responsible for a number of inherited human afflictions.

As scientists came across more and more such genes, a movement grew to sequence the entire human genome—all of the units of hereditary information in the human species. As early as 1986, James Watson began to argue for a government-sponsored project to undertake a sequencing of the human DNA with a view to eventually finding tests, preventive measures, and/or cures for at least five thousand known genetic diseases. Such diseases ranged from cystic fibrosis to cancer, from the fatal nerve degeneration disease known as ALS (Lou Gehrig's disease) to Alzheimer's.

The project would facilitate a search for the genes that caused the potentially lethal disease of the red blood cells known as sickle-cell anemia, the middle-age dementia disorder Huntington's disease, the genes for mental illnesses, alcoholism, drug addiction, and other behavior-related syndromes.

In 1990, Watson succeeded in getting the U.S. Congress to authorize the huge and costly Human Genome Project. The study began with one hundred donors supplying blood samples. But the challenge of sequencing was so vast that the research had to be divided into sections that spread out over sixteen laboratories on five continents. The drive to sequence the human genome was also joined by a private company, which used new methods and machines to speed the project and entered into a race with the public research group.

At the urging of President Bill Clinton, the competing groups finally agreed to cooperate and to coordinate their findings. On June 26, 2000, they announced that they had completed a draft of 90 percent of the human genome, consisting of some 38,000 genes, and published their findings in the scientific literature in February 2001. The Human Genome Project had originally been scheduled to take until 2003 to be completed.

The sequencing of the human DNA was accompanied by the discovery of the genomic structure of many other organisms. They have included certain plants, yeast, viruses, the nematode worm, the fruit fly, and the mouse. The latter has been especially useful in genetic research because so many of the genes in the mouse and the human are the same.

The opportunity to do laboratory experiments on mice in the areas of gene therapy and gene testing has opened many possibilities for the prevention of genetic diseases and for eventual cures. Gene therapy, as practiced in the case of Jesse Gelsinger, may have useful applications in the future even though trials were brought to a halt in 2003.

New efforts to manage the risks of gene therapy, through the use of less dangerous vectors, or viral carriers, to deliver the therapy to the body cells, were announced in April 2004. If the side effects of the delivery system can be reduced, there is hope for new treatments not only for leukemia and "bubble boy" disease but for heart disease, cancer, and rheumatoid arthritis.

The Uses and Consequences of Gene Testing

While safe and effective gene therapy may have to await further investigation, gene testing—the examination of DNA in a blood, other fluid, or tissue sample—has been available for some time, and is both safe and reliable. Its widespread uses include the screening of would-be parents for such genetic diseases as cystic fibrosis, sickle-cell anemia, and Tay-Sachs (a disease that causes mental retardation in infants). About one in twenty-five people carry the gene for cystic fibrosis. The chances that their offspring could suffer from the choking, life-shortening disease, with its abnormal secretions of thick mucus, are not inconsiderable.

Women who are pregnant can be tested to determine whether they are carrying a child who will be born with Down syndrome, and can be given the option to abort early in the pregnancy. Down syndrome affects one in a thousand families. Gene testing is also widely used to screen newborns for abnormalities.

Most cancers appear to be acquired mutations resulting from factors of age and the environment. There are also cancers, however, that clearly run in families and that have been shown to be of genetic origin. One such type is the breast cancer that has been identified as resulting from the presence of the susceptibility gene known as BRCA1.

Only 5 percent to 10 percent of breast cancers are considered to be familial, or genetic. Yet an estimated 600,000 women in the United States are believed to carry the BRCA1 gene and, among those who test positive for it, close to 80 percent are likely to get the disease by the age of sixty-five. While the physical risks of gene testing are minimal, the psychological impact is strong. Testing positive for a known genetic disease often leads to anxiety, depression, and the problem of having to choose a course of action that may be drastic. In the case of women who test positive for genetic breast cancer, many do make the choice to have a double mastectomy—the removal of still healthy breast tissue, which may become cancerous. The procedure falls into the category known as prophylactic surgery, and studies have shown that it prevents cancer in more than 90 percent of cases.

Is There a Case for the Genetic Enhancement of Humans?

A major goal in the application of human genetics is that of preventing and/or curing inherited diseases and disor-

James Watson on Human Genetics

The co-discoverer of the structure of DNA is a strong advocate for the improvement of human life through the application of the genetic knowledge we have gained from his discovery. Although often a controversial figure because of his support of gene testing to detect and deal with abnormalities that can be prevented by means of abortion, he defends his position as follows.

"There are serious diseases no child should be born with. There is no purpose to it. It's all Darwinian—the selection of those who are fit and then the constant generation of new variability. The price of this variability is genetic injustice. What the world of human genetics is trying to do is reduce the level of genetic injustice, not create the perfect human."

Yet Watson continues to be challenged by those who oppose the abortion of children who would be born with Down syndrome or other abnormalities. Others see him as threatening the diversity of the species by eliminating certain human variations, even of a negative nature. Still others accuse him of wanting to limit human creativity because of his advocacy for using genetic testing to rule out the likelihood of passing on to future generations the genes for such familial mental disorders as manic depression. Many geniuses, especially in the arts, have suffered from manic depression. Watson questions, however, whether human misery is ever justified.

Watson persists in his belief that we should direct our own evolution rather than continue to be the victims of the genetic lottery. "One often hears the argument, 'What right do you have to interfere with nature?' But the nature out there isn't the prod-

IN 1962, FRANCIS CRICK (LEFT) AND JAMES WATSON WERE AWARDED THE NOBEL PRIZE FOR THEIR 1953 DISCOVERY OF DNA, WHICH MADE THE SEQUENCING OF GENES POSSIBLE. WATSON STARTED OUT AS A FIERCE ENEMY OF CLONING, BUT NOW TAKES THE OPPOSITE STANCE.

uct of a great design . . . it's just evolution happening. And this evolution depends on random changes and genetic messages, which make some organisms better able to survive and others not that able.

"It would be irresponsible," Watson concludes, "not to direct your evolution if you could, in the sense that you would have a healthy child versus an unhealthy child."

ders, as well as treating acquired injuries and disabilities. Suppose, however, that the scientists of the near future find themselves able to use genetic engineering for purposes that are not solely therapeutic. Suppose they find themselves able to engineer humans to have more attractive bodies, stronger muscles, greater intelligence, sharper memories, and consistently happy moods.

As in the case of human reproductive cloning, parents would have the option of choosing the genetic makeup of their offspring. But instead of creating copies of favored individuals, they would have a wide range of characteristics to select from, characteristics that might not yet exist in any of the clone donors at hand. In other words, the genetic engineering of humans for the purpose of enhancement would mean altering or adding specific genes to the embryo so that a child would be born with characteristics that he or she would otherwise not have had.

Another name for this type of enhancement would be germline engineering, because the new traits would be incorporated into a fertilized human embryo, one that resulted from the union of egg and sperm, otherwise known as germ cells, as opposed to body, or somatic, cells. How would this be done?

As described by author Bill McKibben in his book *Enough: Staying Human in an Engineered Age*, "scientists . . .would probably start with a fertilized embryo a week or so old. They would tease apart the cells of that embryo and then, selecting one, they would add to, delete, or modify some of its genes. They could also insert artificial chromosomes containing predesigned genes."

McKibben continues, "They would then take the cell, place it inside an egg whose nucleus had been removed, and implant the resulting embryo inside a woman. The embryo would, if all went according to plan, grow into a genetically engineered child."

Another name for this product of the advanced genetic age would be a "designer baby."

The prospect of using gene manipulation to either eliminate inherited illnesses and other disadvantages, or to seek to go beyond "wellness" and approach "perfection," requires employing the technology of cloning as well. Cloning is an essential element because, for genetic engineering to work, the manipulated embryonic cells would have to be cultured and tested (via cloning) to make sure that they had received their new genetic messages. The cells that tested positive for received alterations would be the ones to be implanted, thus guaranteeing the birth of a genetically engineered child. The name of the procedure is preimplantation genetic diagnosis (PGD).

Advocates of germline engineering, including the Princeton biologist Lee Silver, see it not only as a way for parents to ensure physical, intellectual, and emotional superiority in their offspring, but as a way to buy them freedom from a host of disadvantageous genetic tendencies. Such negative traits might include obesity, acne, high blood pressure, heart disease, asthma, alcoholism, mental illness, and a predisposition toward cancer.

Going even further, Silver envisions an arbitrarily chosen time in the future—March 15, 2050—when a child-to-be might be designed with a "special gene [that] will provide her with lifelong resistance to infection by the virus that causes AIDS." Silver predicts that by 2050, "no cure for the awful disease has been found, and the only absolute protection comes from the insertion of a resistance gene into the single-cell embryo within twenty-four hours after conception." He agrees that parents must have the financial means to endow their child with this very costly method of inuring her to a worldwide scourge. "Other, less well-off American families," Silver admits, "cannot afford this luxury."

Silver's casual acceptance of a society in which the elitist, so-called GenRich class (genetically enriched members of society) have advantages not open to the non-genetically-engineered Naturals, is only one of the many arguments brought to bear against seeking human perfection through genetic manipulation of the human embryo.

Nor does Silver draw a line between engineering a child who will be genetically fortified against life-threatening cancers, heart disease, and AIDS, and one who is free of facial blemishes and a roly-poly figure. The latter desirable traits are clearly those that go along with physical attractiveness, inborn talents and creativity, and emotional stability. Where then would the wealthy and ambitious parents of the future draw the line between genetic intervention for reasons of health and genetic intervention for the enhancement of appearance, intellect, talents, muscles, memories, and moods?

Arguments against Designer Babies

As in the case of human reproductive cloning, critics of human genetic engineering oppose it on ethical, moral, social, and religious grounds. They see it as an assault on the freedom and dignity of the individual. The designer baby has been robbed of the free genetic expression that characterizes undesigned humans. Instead, it has received qualities that are deemed valuable by its parents, all too likely seeking to fulfill their own ambitions. Critics do not take into account the resentment that some young people might feel if their parents had *not* had the foresight to prevent the inheritance of markedly undesirable traits.

The achievements of the predesigned child, critics add, be they in sports, intellectual pursuits, or artistic eminence, are the result of shortcuts rather than human effort, drive, and eventual mastery. Like the athlete who wins as a result of taking steroids, the designed human who achieves over undesigned individuals can be seen to have done so unfairly. He has also cheated himself, because victory, some say, is something one should earn rather than inherit via implanted genes. On the other hand, we already enhance nature without genetic engineering when we seek plastic surgery, growth hormones, stomach-stapling for obesity, and laser surgery for better eyesight.

There are a variety of social, as well as moral and ethical, arguments against designer babies. The specter of eugenics—the breeding of humans with the aim of perfecting the species—comes to the fore. As in the arguments against human reproductive cloning, is germline engineering the "new" eugenics?

Other critics feel that germline engineering will alter the gene pool. By eliminating or adding genetic traits to the human family, the definition of what it is to be human will gradually change. This long-range view, however, is eclipsed by other problems, such as a growing gap in society based on wealth and power. For the cost of genetically designing one's offspring surely discriminates against parents who cannot afford it. Such discrimination not only creates a super-race versus an underclass; it destroys the social fabric of what might otherwise be an integrated society.

Also, once the race has begun to bring "better" children into the world to ensure their chances of dominance over others, where will it stop? McKibben offers the example of a child born in 2005 who has been given "a state-of-the-art gene job" that will yield ten extra IQ points. "By the time [the child] is five, though, scientists will doubtless have discovered ten more genes linked to intelligence. Now anyone with a platinum card can get twenty IQ points, not to mention a memory boost and a wrinkle-free brow."

By the time McKibben's child has reached her twenties and is ready for the job market, "she's already more or less obsolete—the kids coming out of college just plain have better hardware." McKibben compares germline engineering to an arms race among fiercely competitive world nations, one that "will accelerate endlessly and unstoppably into the future."

Religious thinkers, for the most part, find germline engineering solely for purposes of human enhancement offensive because its arrogance and desire for control defy both God and nature. They feel that giftedness should be derived from natural forces rather than imposed through the intervention of laboratory science.

Writing in *The Atlantic Monthly* on "The Case Against Perfection," political philosopher Michael J. Sandel of Harvard University expresses the view of religionists as follows: "To believe that our talents and powers are wholly our own doing is to misunderstand our place in creation, to confuse our role with God's."

Sandel concludes that "In a social world that prizes mastery and control," parenthood ought to be a "school for humility." Whether from religious or purely moral principles, it would seem that rather than doting on having designer babies parents might consider that "one of the blessings of seeing ourselves as creatures of nature, God, or fortune is that we are not wholly responsible for the way we are."

6
Should We Continue to Clone Animals?

The 1997 announcement of the cloning of Dolly the sheep propelled the world of science and the public toward thinking about a wide range of technological possibilities that bore more directly on humans than on animals. Discussions centered on human reproductive cloning—the making of clone babies—and on the medical uses to which human embryonic stem cells might be put. Cloning also found a place in the field of human genetic engineering, for it was a means of making sure that the selected genetic material had been successfully added to (or altered, or deleted from) the manipulated embryo before its implantation into the uterus.

Animal cloning and the benefits that had been intended through the use of the new technology seemed all but forgotten for the moment. There were, nonetheless, many advantages to be gained from the cloning of animals, and these progressed ever more rapidly once Dolly

The Bovine Cloning Process

1.) Primordial stem cells from 30-day-old calf fetus

2.) Growth-promoting proteins introduced

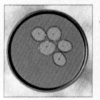

3.) Permanent embryonic stem cells develop

4.) Nucleus of unfertilized egg removed (enucleated)

5.) Cloned stem cell introduced, fused into enucleated oocyte

6.) Cell activated with protein media to promote growth

7.) Cells multiply rapidly

8.) Nucleus of another unfertilized egg removed

9.) Cloned stem cell introduced, fused into enucleated oocyte

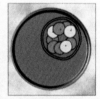

10.) Cloned cells multiply, develop for 7 days...

11.) ... Develop into immature embryo

12.) Embryo transferred to recipient cow; gestates 280 days

The cloned calf is born

THE PROCESS FOR CLONING MILKING COWS IS SHOWN ON A STEP-BY-STEP CHART.

had paved the way. Animal cloning was, and is, a vital tool in medical research and in the delivery of drug therapy for such diseases as hemophilia, cystic fibrosis, and diabetes.

It also continues to promise a supply of donor organs—hearts, kidneys, livers, lungs, the pancreas, and even bone marrow—that could be grown in pigs, for example, and genetically modified for transplant into humans, with reduced chances of rejection by the human immune system.

New York Times reporter Gina Kolata describes in *Clone* how this process would work to supplement donated human organs, of which there is always a shortage to fill the long waiting lists. "Scientists could . . . add human genes . . . in the laboratory, creating pig cells that were coated with human proteins. Then they could make cloned pigs from those cells. Each pig would have organs that looked, to a human immune system, for all the world like a human organ. These organs could be used for transplantation."

Even more effective would be the possibility of implanting the individual patient's own genes into the animal intended to grow the replacement organ. The match in such cases could be so genetically perfect that no immune-system rejection would occur, and it would not be necessary for the organ recipient to take the usual immune-system suppressant drugs. Growing animal organs for use in humans is a transgenic process that involves the introduction of genes from one species into another; the implanting of organs from animals into humans is called xenotransplantation.

Cloning Animals to Expand the Food Supply

Animal cloning has several other applications as well. The Roslin Institute, where the work on Dolly took place in the 1990s, was founded in the 1940s during World War II. One

CLONED CATTLE, LIKE THESE PRODUCED BY ADVANCED CELL TECH-
NOLOGY IN WORCESTER, MASSACHUSETTS, ARE A SOURCE OF IM-
PROVED AGRICULTURAL STOCK FOR MEAT AND MILK PRODUCTION.

of its purposes was to try to improve the agricultural food supply of an embattled Great Britain, which was being blockaded by the German enemy. Over the years much effort went into the development of livestock that was healthier and that produced better meat and milk products.

With the advent of cloning, it has become possible to create superior breeds of beef cattle and dairy animals and to make multiple carbon copies of them using either embryonic or adult cells and gestating them in surrogate mothers. The question is still open, however, as to when food from cloned animals is likely to appear on the market.

Although most consumers were unaware of it, meat and milk products from cloned cattle were sold and eaten in the United States during the late 1980s. The cloned animals of 1988 were produced from embryos, for this was before the advent of Dolly and the development of the 1996 technique of cloning animals from adult cells.

The method used by the scientists of the 1980s was to first try to breed a superior animal. Once they had produced a successful specimen, they would freeze some of the embryos for future cloning in order to make multiple copies. The products of these animals went to market and consumers ate them, unaware of the fact that they were from cloned beef and milk cattle. Nor did the federal Food and Drug Administration (FDA) raise any questions about their safety or even their identification through labeling.

Today, the prospect of eating food from cloned animals raises a number of questions. Food safety experts and consumers are concerned about the health aspects of eating cloned animals, especially those created from adult cells, as in the case of Dolly. Some advocates of putting cloned animal products on the market say that it makes no difference whether the animal resulted from embryonic or adult-cell cloning. But it is unlikely that many people would have wanted to sample the meat of Dolly the sheep, in view of her advanced aging accompanied by the onset of lung disease and arthritis.

In addition to being much more aware of food safety today than in the 1980s, the public is also squeamish about the idea of cloning animals for food because of the connected and controversial issue of human reproductive cloning. Nor is it likely that large numbers of cloned animal products will come to market in the immediate future. *The New York Times* reports, "There are now only several hundred cloned cattle, for instance, out of the nation's total of about 100 million, so experts do not expect an immediate influx of food from cloned animals if they were allowed. Cloning an animal can cost about $20,000, much too expensive to make an animal just for its milk or meat. . . . Instead the main use would be to make copies of prized animals for breeding."

Yet the FDA has not ruled out the possibility that beef, milk, butter, cheese, and ice cream from cloned cattle may be served up to the American public some time in the near future. Nor, as of spring 2005, had it made any decision as to whether or not such products would have to be labeled.

Cloning Animals to Save Endangered Species

Dead as the dodo—this is the expression that is commonly used to describe animal species that once roamed the earth and that were completely wiped out over time through a variety of causes, never to be reproduced. The dodo was a flightless bird about the size of a turkey that lived on islands in the Indian Ocean. Explorers who reached the islands in the 1600s brought pigs and monkeys that attacked the birds. Sailors probably killed off most of the dodoes, and the last dodo was believed to have died in 1681.

The dodo is one of numerous species that became extinct as a result of environmental and climatic changes, the inability to adapt to them, over-hunting, and, above all, the encroachment of humans into their habitats. Such species range from the dinosaurs of up to 65 million years ago to the estimated hundred or so plant and animal varieties that presently die out every day.

Nor does the loss of a single species tell the entire story of biological change and ecological disruption. Be it the dinosaur, the woolly mammoth, the giant sloth, the North American passenger pigeon, or the Tasmanian tiger, each organism is connected to a much wider web of natural life. The organism's demise breaks a chain that is vital to the biodiversity of the earth.

In spite of the premise in the novel and movie, *Jurassic Park*, that dinosaurs could once again walk the earth, it so far appears that the DNA in the dead cells of extinct species is so badly decomposed that it could not be recovered for purposes of renewal.

In 1999, hope was briefly held out for the possibility

of cloning a woolly mammoth from a frozen carcass that was discovered in Russia's Siberian region, using cells extracted from the animal's bones or tissue. Scientists contemplated recreating the woolly mammoth, which had been extinct for over ten thousand years, by inserting the nucleus from one of its cells into the enucleated egg of an elephant, and then implanting the embryo into the elephant's uterus. However, the apparently well-preserved mammoth tissue proved to have lost its DNA integrity and thus its genetic code through repeated thawing and freezing cycles over the eons. Similarly, hopes for cloning a Tasmanian tiger pup preserved in alcohol since 1866 in Australia have been dashed because its DNA is in such poor condition.

The advent of cloning has, however, apparently made it possible to save some animals that are today on the endangered list and possibly on the verge of extinction. An early success story was that of the cloning of a gaur, a one-ton oxlike animal native to India, Indochina, and Southeast Asia that had long been hunted by the native populations for its hide, horns, and hooves. By the late 1990s, it was estimated that there were only about 36,000 members of the valuable species of bovine left in the world.

In 1997, Advanced Cell Technology (ACT) of Worcester, Massachusetts, collected skin cells from a gaur that had recently died, implanted the nuclei in enucleated eggs taken from dairy cows, and merged the two via electric shock. ACT then allowed the cloned embryos to grow in the laboratory until they reached the blastocyst stage, and implanted them in the uteruses of dairy cows.

Although ACT began with 692 injected eggs, only 81 grew to blastocysts, only eight cows became pregnant with gaur fetuses, and only one surviving live birth resulted. The baby gaur was named Noah. Although he later died of an infection, his creation was hailed as a milestone. The project also made evident the necessity of finding enucleated eggs and surrogate mothers from a domesticated species when attempting to clone wild animals.

ACT repeated this type of project in 2003 when it crossed another endangered wild bovine species, the banteng of the forests of Southeast Asia, with domesticated Angus cows. Other successes have included producing a declining variety of African wildcat by cross-species cloning with an ordinary housecat, who became its birth mother. Similarly, it has been shown that wild varieties of antelopes, sheep, and deer that are deemed to be on the endangered list can be preserved by means of interspecies transfer and the use of domesticated varieties as surrogate mothers.

Hope is held out for preserving other dwindling species such as the cheetah and the tiger, if suitable domestic species can be found to provide enucleated eggs and surrogate mothers. Meanwhile, animal biologists and environmentalists press for a growing network of laboratories in which the frozen body cells of endangered species could be preserved to prevent their joining the dinosaur and the dodo on the extinction list.

Experimental Animal Cloning Since Dolly the Sheep

In October 1997, almost on the heels of the announcement of Dolly's birth, scientists at the University of Hawaii managed to produce the first cloned mouse, a female to whom they gave the name of Cumulina. The so-called "Honolulu technique" of cloning involved the nuclear-transfer method. Using a body cell from an adult mouse, the Hawaii team injected its nucleus into an egg from which the nucleus had been removed, and activated the egg so that its new genetic material would be reproduced by implantation in the uterus of a surrogate mother. Another successful experiment, which produced the first cloned male mouse, named Fibro, followed.

Because of the genomic similarity between humans and mice, mice are extremely valuable in laboratory research aimed at testing products and procedures with applications to human health problems. The cloned mice proved highly useful in experiments aimed at the treatment of Parkinson's and other neurological diseases and disorders in humans.

In Parkinsonism, patients lose the brain cells that control muscle movements, resulting in stiffness and jerkiness. On September 21, 2003, BBC News reported that "cells taken from cloned mouse embryos have been used to successfully treat a condition similar to Parkinson's disease in humans." Further, implanting embryonic stem cells in the mouse brain that were "a perfect genetic match for the transplant recipient" removed "the need for extra treatments to suppress the immune system."

It is encouraging to know that embryonic stem cells cloned from the mouse "patient" were able to grow healthy new tissue in the reported experiment, which was conducted at Memorial Sloan-Kettering Cancer Center in New York. Unfortunately, however, there are still many obstacles in the way of applying this treatment to humans.

Among them is the politically controversial issue of producing human stem cells for therapeutic research. There are also scientific problems to be solved with regard to the safe and effective implantation of such cells into the human brain.

While the early efforts to clone mice encountered incidences of premature death due to liver damage, tumors, and pneumonia, experimenters at the Massachusetts Institute of Technology announced in February 2004 that they had come up with a new breed of cloned mouse. It was healthier and hardier than the animals produced in 1997. Instead of using the nucleus of a body cell, such as a skin cell, in the nuclear-transfer procedure, Rudolf Jaenisch at MIT's Whitehead Institute used the nucleus of a nerve cell from the mouse's nose as a means of introducing the DNA of the animal into the enucleated egg.

Under the heading Mouse Cloning Achievement, it was reported that "the resulting embryos developed into mature, fertile cloned mice."

The successful cloning of monkeys was also first achieved in 1997, when two rhesus monkeys named Neti and Ditto were produced at the Oregon Primate Research Center in Beaverton, Oregon. The method used was not identical to the nuclear-transfer technology that produced Dolly because embryonic rather than body cells were the source of the two monkeys' genetic identity.

Less than three years later, on January 14, 2000, an article appearing in *Science* magazine announced the birth of a monkey named Tetra that resulted entirely from the process of embryo-splitting—also known as artificial twinning—which had been used for some time on cattle. Following a procedure similar to that of in vitro fertilization, "scientists at the Oregon Regional Primate Research Center began by taking an egg from the mother monkey and sperm from the father monkey and then mixing them together to create a fertilized egg. Once the embryo had grown into eight cells, the scientists divided the embryo into four identical embryos consisting of two cells each. These four embryos were then implanted into four potential monkey mothers."

Although only one live birth, named Tetra from the Greek word for four, resulted from the experiment, researchers saw it as a reliable means of producing a line of identical primates that could be used to test new treatments for AIDS, cancer, and heart disease in humans. In spite of the low success rate, scientists continue to pursue monkey cloning via embryo-splitting or similar genetically assured methods because monkey biology is more similar to human biology than mouse biology is, making monkeys more useful for clinical testing.

Back on the domestic-animal cloning front, April 1999 saw the announcement of the birth of the first cloned goats, all females. The eldest of the three, Mira, was born late in 1998 and her two sisters a month later. Like Dolly the sheep, the cloned goats were designed to be "living drug factories," or "pharming" animals. In this case, the clones were produced to advance the possibility of increasing the supply of goat's milk containing a human factor that helps blood to clot. For humans with hemophilia and other bleeding disorders, surgical procedures without the administration of the clotting factor are extremely dangerous.

To create Mira and her sisters, researchers used a goat embryo that already contained the human clotting factor rather than an adult cell as in the case of Dolly. The genetic material in the embryonic cell "was then fused with an empty egg taken from another goat and activated to make it think it had been fertilised [sic]." Again, the success rate was low because the research team from Tufts University and Louisiana State University "used 285 eggs to get the three live clones."

Efforts to clone goats from adult cells by Chinese researchers in the year 2000 resulted in disappointment at first. The animals appeared to suffer from various problems and died soon after birth. However, one goat, named Yangyang, cloned from an adult cell at the China Science and Technology University in Shaanxi Province that year, did survive. On February 8, 2004, it was announced that Yangyang was not only still in good health but had become the great-grandmother of a female kid.

The 1998 reproduction of goats via cloning was followed by the birth of the first litter of cloned pigs in March 2000. Pigs are valued for the potential of transplanting

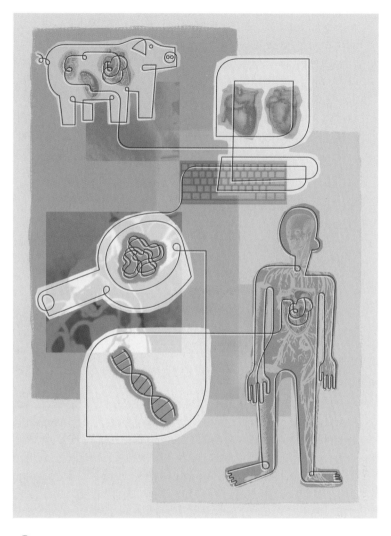

GENETICALLY MODIFIED ORGANS, SUCH AS PIG HEARTS, HAVE THE PROM-ISE OF SUPPLYING DONOR ORGANS FOR HUMANS.

their organs, which are similar in size to those of humans, into patients requiring replacement heart valves, as well as a kidney, a liver, or a pancreas. In April 2001, PPL Therapeutics, the Scotland-based company that had sponsored the cloning of Dolly at the Roslin Institute, announced that it had produced a litter of five transgenic piglets—animals that had had a foreign human gene inserted into their DNA. The purpose was to try to engineer pigs whose organs would have a reduced chance of being rejected if they were transplanted into humans.

The transgenic pigs were named Millie, Christa, Alexis, Carrel, and Dotcom. The creation of a line of cloned pigs with potentially people-friendly organs appeared to be a significant development in helping to alleviate the long waiting lists for organ replacement among human patients. Pigs are relatively easy to breed, and experimenting with farmyard animals does not seem to provoke as much outcry as experiments done on primates such as apes and monkeys. Nonetheless the cross-species transplant, also known as xenotransplantation, does awaken fears that putting pig organs into people could give rise to new viruses that would be dangerous to human recipients. There are also questions as to the safety of using organs from cloned animals that might appear to be normal but later prove defective.

What about Cloning Pet Animals?

The successes, although sometimes limited, in producing clones of mice, monkeys, goats, and pigs, in the years between 1997 and 2001, led to a growing interest in the possibility of cloning such pet animals as cats and dogs.

Unlike the earlier animal cloning projects—undertaken for the purpose of studying cures for human disease, delivering pharmaceuticals, or supplying organs for transplant—pet cloning is driven by personal motives. It more closely resembles human reproductive cloning, for its purpose is to attempt to recreate a beloved cat or dog that is a carbon copy of the dead or dying pet in appearance. Pet owners also hope that the animal clone will have the same personality and behavioral characteristics as the pet they are trying to reproduce.

As early as 1998, scientists at Texas A&M University declared their intention to clone a pet dog named Missy. The eleven-year-old animal was a mix of Border collie and husky, and was owned by a wealthy, anonymous American couple. It was estimated that the cost of creating a clone of Missy would be $2.3 million.

While there have so far been no reported successes with cloning dogs, it was announced in February 2002 that a cloned domestic cat had been produced at Texas A&M University. The kitten, given the name Cc—which stands for carbon copy—was the result of nuclear-transfer technology. The DNA of a tortoiseshell, or calico, cat was injected into an enucleated egg, which was then implanted in the uterus of a surrogate mother that happened to be a tabby cat.

The clone kitten is a genetic match of her calico donor mother, but does not resemble her exactly because "the pattern on cats' coats is only partly genetically determined—it also depends on other factors during development."

Of eighty-seven embryos implanted in surrogate animals, Cc was the only cat clone to survive, indicating that the success rate remains rather low, as it does for the cloning of other animal species. Nonetheless, the birth of the first cloned kitten was certain to set up a clamor for more carbon copies of animal pets.

Cloning the Rabbit, the Mule, the Horse, and the Rat

The first successful rabbit clone was announced in March 2002, a month after the appearance of Cc, the cat clone. Rabbits naturally reproduce rapidly, becoming sexually

Cc, OR CARBON COPY, WAS THE NAME GIVEN TO THE FIRST CLONED CAT. HER BIRTH WAS ANNOUNCED BY TEXAS A&M UNIVERSITY IN FEBRUARY 2002.

mature in four months and undergoing a pregnancy that lasts only one month. So it would seem that there was little need to increase the rabbit population by means of cloning.

However, the aim of the French scientists responsible for the work on rabbits was to create another animal—in addition to sheep, goats, and cows—that is capable of producing pharmaceutically useful proteins in its milk. The team at the Agronomy Research Institute in France points out that "A sheep would produce several hundred litres [sic] [of milk], but 20 to 40 rabbits would give you the same amount."

The researchers also point out that identical cloned rabbits with certain genes "knocked out" could be useful in laboratory research seeking to treat human diseases by mimicking them in large numbers of rabbits.

The cloned rabbits were produced from adult donor cells via the nuclear-transfer method, and the embryos that resulted from the fusion were implanted in surrogate mother rabbits. As has so often been the case, however, the success rate was low. Hundreds of fused embryos resulted in only six live births, and two of the rabbits died soon afterward. An encouraging sign has been that the four surviving rabbit clones matured and reproduced normally.

The year 2003 saw the return to large-animal cloning with the birth of the first mule and the first horse. The cloning of a mule is a special achievement because the mule is a hybrid animal that cannot reproduce itself naturally. It results from crossing a male donkey with a mare, or female horse, and is itself sterile.

The mule born on May 4, 2003 resulted from a five-year effort led by scientists at the University of Idaho, and was named Idaho Gem. The method used entailed fusing a body cell from a forty-five-day-old mule fetus with an enu-

What's Wrong with Pet Cloning?

Pet cloning enthusiasts defend the right of those who can afford the astronomical costs to have their favorite animals copied and, not surprisingly, a number of private companies have sprung up in the United States and elsewhere. Such companies promise to store a beloved animal's DNA for a given charge, and to recreate that animal at an additional cost when feasible.

Nor are pet owners discouraged by the knowledge that, as in the theoretical case of human reproductive cloning, environmental factors may intervene to make a pet's personality and behavior quite different from that of its donor parent. Further, they approve the idea of pet cloning because animals would not be likely to suffer the psychological damage that humans might, knowing they had been created in a forebear's genetic image.

In the wake of the cloning of Cc, however, the Humane Society of the United States (HSUS) issued a statement opposing pet cloning "because it is dangerous for the animals involved, it serves no compelling social purpose, and it threatens to add to the pet overpopulation problem."

The February 14, 2002 release of the HSUS added, "Cloning animals strips away the altruistic component behind petkeeping and reduces the experience to one of selfishness. There is something wonderful about providing hope and homes for animals in need."

Finally, while some pet owners have such close bonds with their animals that they would seek to recreate them at almost any cost, it is ironic that "a break in this bond is the leading cause of pet overpopulation, which leads to the deaths of millions of animals each year." In other words, the Humane Society is saying that it seems pointless to add to the overcrowded pet population through cloning when so many pets are added to it through neglect and abandonment.

cleated horse egg. The resulting embryo was then implanted in a surrogate mare.

One of the purposes of cloning the first mule was to develop a step toward the cloning of other equine animals, especially horses. As a result, the birth of Prometea, the world's first cloned horse, took place on May 28, 2003, at the Laboratory of Reproductive Technology in Cremona, Italy, and was announced on August 6.

The Italian scientists reported that they had used the nuclear-transfer method, taking a skin cell from a Haflinger mare, fusing it with an enucleated egg from the same mare, and then implanting the resulting embryo in the donor mare. Prometea, the foal that was born eleven months later, was thus both the daughter and the sister of the mare that bore her.

Although the success rate was low (the 841 embryos created resulted in only one live birth), horse cloning has a number of possible applications. It could allow for the survival of rare and endangered species of wild horses. It could also allow male racehorses that have been castrated to improve their temperaments and—known as geldings—to be reproduced. Geldings cannot make their own sperm, but they could "father" genetically identical copies by contributing skin cells. Their foals would revert to their pre-castrated genetic makeup and could then be used as studs.

The year 2003 concluded with the first successful cloning of the laboratory rat by researchers in France and in China. The announcement of the birth of Ralph, one of the first rat clones, was made on September 25, 2003, by scientists at two cooperating French research institutes.

While mice were first cloned using the nuclear-transfer technique as early as 1997, the cloning of the rat was delayed due to a peculiarity in the animal's ovulation process. Rat eggs become activated so soon after leaving

Could We Create a Breed of Champion Racehorses?

Once the success rate for cloning horses improved, would owners of racehorses begin to clone champions to try to win as many races as possible?

Such a practice would not be acceptable to the 110-year-old Jockey Club, which is responsible for the registration of all North American thoroughbred horses. The Club has issued a ruling against allowing cloned horses to compete in its races. Nor does it permit the entry of horses created by in vitro fertilization or other assisted reproductive techniques. Early in 2003, the American Quarter Horse Association announced the adoption of similar rules.

So far, however, the Olympics and many other horse events—including dressage, jumping, and harness racing—have not issued any rules against allowing cloned animals to compete. So offers of prize money may indeed spur owners of superior animals to clone them.

What happens, however, when genetically identical championship horses run, for example, in the same racing event? Do they all finish at the same time? Not necessarily, according to Ernest Bailey, an expert in horse genetics at the University of Kentucky. Bailey explained that even clones of a champion racehorse such as Secretariat, the 1973 Triple Crown winner, would not cross the finish line at the same time because a number of environmental factors—and especially interaction with trainers and jockeys—would make for many variations in response.

On the other hand, if all the horses in the race were potential winners, what would happen to the excitement of betting on a favorite that might come from behind?

the ovaries that there is very little time available to introduce the genetic material from the donor rat into the enucleated egg. Chinese scientists described in a paper published online by the journal *Science* how they used a chemical in the form of a protein inhibitor to stabilize the rat eggs at a key moment. Thus they were able to successfully create the embryos that were implanted in the surrogate mothers.

With an effective cloning technology established for rats, researchers hope to be able to manipulate the animals genetically in order to mimic in them a variety of human illnesses. If diabetes, hypertension, heart disease, neurological disorders, and cancer can be mirrored in laboratory rats designed with special genetic changes, it should be possible to test drugs and other therapies that may be of benefit to humans with those diseases.

Animal Cloning: Right or Wrong?

Defenders of animal cloning argue that it is justified, especially when practiced for purposes such as preserving endangered species and extending research for the treatment and cure of human diseases and disorders. Even religious authorities often see justification for the practice, for using animals to pursue medical advances appears to follow in the path of Christ's example advocating healing, as well as feeding the hungry.

Adherents of the teachings of the Bible also point out that God gave humans dominion over the rest of creation, including the animals (*Genesis* 1:28: "over every living thing that moveth upon the earth.") He also granted humans the right to kill animals (*Genesis* 9:3: "Every moving thing that liveth shall be meat for you.")

Animal rights activists, however, and animal liberationists see animal cloning, as well as the killing of animals for food, clothing, and traditional medical research, as morally and ethically wrong because it is intrinsically selfish and cruel.

With regard to animal cloning, their chief objections have to do with the suffering and health risks to the animals involved. Baby calves, for example, who have been created by cloning are sometimes so big that they cannot be born naturally, thus causing intense pain, if not death, to their surrogate mothers.

Another example is that of pigs who have been given human genes so that their organs might be used for xeno-transplantation. Such animals have developed bone and joint problems as a result of the manipulation of their DNA. Similarly, the earlier-attempted genetic manipulation of pigs to make them leaner—and therefore their meat more appealing to consumers—resulted in the animals' developing ulcers and lameness.

Peter Singer, Professor of Bioethics at Princeton University and a leading animal liberationist, tries to balance the good that animal cloning may do for humans "without discounting the sufferings of the animals merely because they are animals, that is, not members of our species. Pain is pain, no matter what the species of the being who feels it."

With regard to the production of "therapeutic proteins in the milk of genetically modified sheep or cattle," Singer writes the following: "If such products will be much less expensive than existing products, and will hence be affordable to people who otherwise would have died without them, then the infliction of a degree of distress on animals could be defended, if it were kept to the minimum necessary for research."

Clearly Singer is trying to find a way through the maze of biotechnological advances of the past twenty years and especially since the birth of Dolly and the mapping of the

THE FIRST CLONED CALF PRODUCED IN LATIN AMERICA WAS BORN IN BRAZIL IN 2001, AND WAS PHOTOGRAPHED A YEAR LATER AS A MATURE ANIMAL.

human genome. He concludes that, with regard to each of these breakthroughs, "we need to make decisions about the many different issues it raises . . . with less haste, with more careful thought, and with a greater awareness of the ethical obligations we have to nonhuman animals, as well as to human beings."

7

What Is the Future of the Genetic Revolution?

A look back at animal cloning since the birth of Dolly is impressive in terms of the increasing number of species that scientists have been able to duplicate and the technological obstacles that researchers have been able to overcome. Although success rates remain comparatively low in terms of live births and healthy animals among the most recent cloning achievements, it is likely that abnormalities will begin to fall off and success rates for the newer animal clones will rise.

Does this mean that, as a result, the advent of human reproductive cloning as a routine procedure will draw closer? Or has the prospect of merely duplicating humans already been superseded by the more sophisticated technology of redesigning humans through germline engineering?

Proponents of the latter, such as Gregory Stock, director of the Program on Medicine, Technology, and Society at the School of Medicine at the University of California at Los Angeles, sees the genetic revolution as yielding much more than carbon copies of existing humans. In *Redesigning Humans: Our Inevitable Genetic Future*, Stock writes that our expanding knowledge of the human genome has given us the tools to change the very nature of "what it means to be human." Going even further, he asserts that, "*Homo sapiens* is not the final word in the primate revolution."

Stock sees the human race advancing via a series of steps and over a period of decades to what he calls "our evolutionary future," putting us "on the cusp of profound biological change." How will this change be accomplished? Already, we are practicing embryo selection as a result of genetic testing, and we have employed the techniques of in vitro fertilization to work with embryos in the laboratory. Synthetic or artificial chromosomes have already been used in mice, Stock tells us, as a better way of regulating gene manipulation in humans versus the more hit-and-miss application of natural genes. "Auxiliary chromosomes may not be the only way of achieving workable, complex germline manipulation, but they give us an idea of the level of sophistication we may one day attain in modifying human genetics."

In direct opposition to advocates of human germline engineering are those critics who see tampering with our genetic makeup as creating a self-designed posthuman race that may eventually be destructive of humankind as we currently know it. They question the advisability of treating humans like the genetically modified varieties of tomatoes, corn, soybeans, potatoes, and other crops that were developed starting in the 1980s. These genetically modified products now flood the market, threatening to overwhelm the food supply and to contaminate with their transgenic pollens the fields in which conventional, or natural, crops are being grown.

Should We Make Humans Better?

In his book, *Enough: Staying Human in an Engineered Age*, technology writer and ethicist Bill McKibben questions the wisdom of "leaping across thresholds" based on the belief that the beneficial medical and scientific advances of the past two hundred years demand that every new advance be applied as well. "While the jump to modern medicine," McKibben writes, "may have freed us from many ills, the next leap to human genetic manipulation will imprison us in a house of distorting mirrors.

"That's how thresholds work: up to a certain point something is good, and past that point there's trouble. . . . Judging when you've reached this 'enough point' is, admittedly, no easy trick. You might stop short and miss some real improvement; you might overshoot and hit some wall. . . . Our food has been genetically modified, which makes us uneasy; our children are about to be, which should make us cringe."

McKibben looks, too, at the implications for society of human germline engineering. Not wanting to deny their offspring the advantages of being taller, more muscular, handsomer, smarter, and emotionally more stable, most parents will stretch their limits financially to produce genetically superior stock. Undeniably, however, the gap between rich and poor within a nation and among richer and poorer nations of the world will divide the biological future of humankind into two distinct groups.

McKibben reminds us that "a sixth of the American population lacks health insurance of any kind—they can't afford to go to a doctor for a *checkup*. And much of the rest of the world is far worse off. If we can't afford the fifty cents a person it would take to buy bed nets to protect most of Africa from malaria, it is unlikely we will extend to anyone but the top tax bracket these latest forms of genetic technology."

Nonetheless, the arguments rage on between those futurists who advocate redesigning humans and those who oppose it with the cry of "enough." UCLA's Stock tells us that "the coming opportunities in germinal choice technology far outweigh the risks. What is more, a free-market environment with real individual choice, modest oversight, and robust mechanisms to learn quickly from mistakes" will help us achieve our goals.

Stock believes that, "unlike nuclear weapons," the technologies of cloning, germline engineering, and genetically altered foods "will be forgiving; they carry no threat of imminent destruction to multitudes of innocent bystanders."

McKibben, on the other hand, not only deeply questions the safety, the potential abuses, and the moral, political, and social issues connected with altering the genetic nature of humankind. He also wonders what redesigning ourselves will turn us into. "If you didn't know how *you* felt, or if you felt how you did because your rejiggered cells were pumping out designer proteins," who would you really be? In other words, if we change the human race can we ever regain its humanity?

"Once we start down the path of turning ourselves into machines, of writing ineradicable programs for our proteins," McKibben observes, "there will be no way, and no reason, to turn back." What McKibben is saying is that our programming will become who we are.

Could Germline Engineering Defeat Death?

Unwilling to let go of the promise of making humans better, advocates of genetic intervention tease us with the prospect of offering us not only healthy and highly superior lives but a life span that would exceed and perhaps even double the present seventy-five or eighty years.

"A sad irony of life," writes Stock, "is that brutal decay is the fate in store for each of us lucky enough to live

FRENCHWOMAN JEANNE CALMENT, THE WORLD'S LONGEST-LIVED
HUMAN, DIED IN 1997 AT THE AGE OF 122.

long enough to reach it." No matter to what degree humans may aspire to healthier lifestyles and seek medical interventions, the bare truth is that senescence, or aging, is built into our body cells. Telomeres—the repeated units of DNA at the ends of the chromosomes in the cells' nuclei—begin to break down. As they do so, the tips of the chromosomes break off and they begin to unravel.

This phenomenon was believed to be responsible for the premature death of Dolly the sheep, who lived roughly half of her normal span. The current maximum human life span is believed to be 115 to 120. The longest-lived known human, Jeanne Calment, of France, died in 1997 at the age of 122.

Suppose, however, that a gene to prevent our aging cells from self-destructing could be implanted in human embryos. Instead of dying off with age, our cells could be instructed to renew themselves. Would any technology resulting from the genetic revolution be more in demand?

Already, as early as 1990, scientists approximately doubled the life spans of fruit flies and roundworms through gene manipulation. Results, however, were applicable only to species that live for very short periods. A 50 percent extension of the life of the roundworm meant that it lived for three weeks instead of two. Testing on mammals would probably be necessary to see if physical decay in humans could be held back.

The mouse, with a three-year or slightly longer life span, is a likely subject for the next step in germline engineering to postpone death. Primates, such as the lemur, which normally lives fifteen years, could then be tested.

Assuming that positive results were obtained and that germline intervention could take the human life span into the realm of 150 to 200, what would then be some of the social problems of a non-dying population? Surely we would have to limit the birth rate to avoid the specter of

Becoming Immortal

The visionary biotechnologist, Stanley Shostak, proposes in his book *Becoming Immortal: Combining Cloning and Stem-Cell Therapy* that human beings can achieve immortality.

Shostak theorizes that because humans are born with the precursors of death—or cells with finite life—already at play in their bodies, changes must be introduced no later than the pre-puberty years. Once humans begin adolescence, their germ cells (eggs and spermatozoa) advance the aging process of their somatic, or body, cells.

Therefore, says Shostak, preadolescence is the time to replace rudimentary germ cells with stem cells, by implanting stem-cell generators into the bodies of the young. These generators would each consist of a cloned blastocyst that would continue to produce embryonic stem cells, acting as a source of cellular renewal and regeneration, in perpetuity.

At what age would Shostak's preadolescents have to be equipped with the gift of immortality? Shostak chooses the physiological age of about eleven. Although he admits that this is "a stage before they are completely developed and mature," it is also a time "at which life is full of excitement, experience, learning, adventure, and, above all, meaning. . . . Such individuals would be close to adulthood and capable of living a relatively fulfilling life . . . albeit not reproducing. Immortal, these human beings would be forever young, never fully grown or sexually mature, but never aging."

With regard to the ethical and moral aspects of choosing to give one's child an immortality that involves sterility and remaining forever at the physiological age of eleven, Shostak admits that he can imagine the bringing of "wrongful immortality" suits against parents. He also admits that some parents might immortalize their children for "no more complicated reason than 'keeping up with the Joneses'."

On the other hand, Shostak sees immortalizing one's children as a means of guaranteeing an unending line of descendants, who may, for all we know, gain enough experience over the endless eons to "solve the remaining problems of life."

With regard to familial and social aspects, there is the question of how mortals and immortals will interact. How will immortals deal with the deaths of mortals among their loved ones and friends, and how will those who are living finite lives feel toward the immortals among them?

Will immortals even find their lives meaningful and stimulating enough to want to go on living forever? In other words . . . what price immortality?

severe planetary overcrowding. Surely there would be elitist divisions between the longevity-enhanced and those who were still destined to die in their seventies and eighties. Lastly, if living to 200 is good, is living to 800 better? Would some of us become greedy for immortality itself?

In response to those who would advocate the prolonging of human life toward extreme longevity, or even promote fanciful means of making humans immortal, McKibben writes the following. "Objecting even slightly to immortality is a little like arguing against ice cream—eternal life has only been humanity's great dream ever since the moment we became conscious. And yet we've never had to deal with the possibility that we might actually be able to bring some version of it into being."

Assuming that such a feat might be possible, McKibben examines the fact that human beings are the only species on Earth that lives with the knowledge that physical death awaits. "Death's overpowering reality," McKibben admits, "drives some of us to embrace various creeds, or to mummify bodies, or to jog. Some of us try to achieve glory so our names will be 'kept alive'. . . . For every person eating and drinking and making merry in the face of death, another is abstaining, hovering around the vitamin aisle at the health food store. Death is us."

Yet, McKibben wonders what meaning life would have if it were endless, stretching flatly into the future, removing the meaning of time, and robbing the present of any urgency toward initiative, accomplishment, achievement. To those who want to stop time and its limitations on human life, McKibben questions whether there would be joy in such a life or whether the "the joy of it—the meaning of it—will melt away like ice cream on an August afternoon." His conclusion is that, although the new technologies may indeed continue to taunt us with their possibilities, "immortality is a fool's goal. Living must be enough for us, not living forever."

Summing Up the Debate on Cloning and Beyond

A final look at the technologies spawned by the genetic revolution leaves us with questions and controversies regarding each of the developments and possibilities it has brought about.

Although the widely debated issue of human reproductive cloning has taken a back seat to that of stem-cell research and therapeutic cloning in recent years, is it possible that somebody somewhere will soon produce, or already has produced, a human clone? Although the use of this technology (known as nuclear transfer) as it might be applied to humans was deeply frowned upon by Ian Wilmut, the creator of Dolly, and his colleagues—as well as many other scientists and bioethicists—determined advocates of human cloning are still out there.

Rael, the founder of Clonaid, continues to assert via its Web site that new clone babies are being clandestinely created right now in undisclosed locations and born in countries that are none the wiser as to their biological origin.

Meanwhile, however, even strong advocates of human reproductive cloning, such as Princeton molecular biologist Lee Silver, have turned their attention to therapeutic cloning. This potentially beneficial technology, involving the creation of human embryos via nuclear transfer, holds the promise of producing a generous supply of stem cells. These cells, because they are undifferentiated, are capable of developing into any of the body's tissues and organs, thus treating or curing a variety of human diseases and disabilities.

As a result, advocacy for stem-cell research has increased in intensity. Victims of paralysis resulting from severe spinal cord injury, such as the actor Christopher Reeve, urged prompt action to revoke President Bush's August 2001 ban limiting the availability of federally funded stem-cell lines (or colonies) so that the regeneration of damaged nerves may be attempted. However, the president, who was reelected in November 2004, and many others, view the harvesting of stem cells for therapeutic purposes as a form of murder because it involves destroying an embryo that has the potential to become a human life.

Other figures in the public eye also urge that stem-cell research be allowed to continue under the auspices of government funding. They include Nancy Reagan and Ron Reagan, the wife and the son of former president Ronald Reagan, who died in June 2004, a victim for ten years of Alzheimer's disease. Afflicted brain cells, such as those causing Alzheimer's disease and Parkinson's disease, are believed to be capable of regeneration through stem-cell therapy. A hopeful development to advocates of stem-cell therapy was the November 2004 passage in the state of California of Proposition 71, appropriating $3 billion for stem-cell research in the state. Also, private corporations and research centers are free to produce and experiment with embryonic stem cells.

Yet another result of the genetic revolution is the issue of human genetic engineering, through gene testing, gene therapy, and germline manipulation. Gene testing for prenatal screening of inherited diseases has proved to be relatively safe and accurate as a diagnostic tool. However, it has led to much controversy in cases where abnormalities are detected and the issue of abortion comes to the fore.

Gene therapy—the treatment of disease by implanting healthy genes to replace defective ones in humans with existing conditions—has proven so far to be experimental and, in certain cases on record, dangerous and even fatal. As a result, its application remains in limbo.

Germline engineering—the enhancement of humans through genetic manipulation of the embryo—for the purpose not only of eliminating inherited diseases but of creating a race of designer offspring, superior to their peers in every way, is the newest wrinkle in the genetic revolution. It has led to heated debate about the very nature of humankind in terms of ethics, morality, human biology, and the global society of the future.

Two eminent figures in the field of medicine have had the following to say regarding the efforts of the proponents of the new enhancement technologies to improve the human species. Leon Eisenberg, professor emeritus of Social Medicine, Harvard Medical School, calls such ideas "biologic nonsense." He advances the view that "pseudo-biology trivializes ethics and distracts our attention from real moral issues, the ways in which the genetic potential of humans born into impoverished environments today is stunted and thwarted. To improve our species, no biologic sleight of hand is needed. Had we the moral commitment to provide every child with what we desire for our own, what a flowering of humankind there would be."

A similar view is taken by Sherwin B. Nuland, clinical professor of surgery at Yale University, bioethicist, and author of *How We Die: Reflections on Life's Final Chapter*, as well as other significant writings on medical issues in our society. With regard to genetic enhancement technologies, Nuland cautions us as follows. "If for no other reason, our society should at least pause briefly to think about its motivations for plunging forward without due consideration of the range of possible consequences or of the immediate financial cost of the research in a time of limited resources."

Is it our goal to attempt to "exist" in offspring that are genetically carbon copies of us, via reproductive cloning, or to remain youthful beyond our years or even live forever, via germline engineering? Nuland sees such fancies as resulting from "the glib predictions of overzealous researchers, keen votaries [who] have uncritically hailed the future of genetic studies."

A MAN IN BERLIN CYCLES PAST A GREEN PARTY ELECTION POSTER
SHOWING ROWS OF SMILING FACES OF U.S. PRESIDENT GEORGE W.
BUSH WITH THE CAPTION, "YOU DECIDE—DON'T GIVE CLONING A
CHANCE." THE GREEN PARTY TARGETED BUSH FOR HIS POSITION
AGAINST CLONING, BUT HE WON REELECTION IN THE UNITED STATES
IN NOVEMBER 2004.

He tells us that "the prevailing mood of our time is self-absorption, and its natural extension, narcissism." Examples are all around us—the emphasis on the youth culture, on personal fulfillment, on the development of human potential via genetic manipulation, even on the pursuit of immortality by this promised means.

Somewhere along the way, however, Nuland tells us, our self-absorption and vanity have clouded our good judgment, and led us into immaturity and foolishness. "Knowing a lot of things does not make us any less foolish. Mere information is only the beginning of knowledge, and even knowledge does not of itself lead to maturity, nor does it guarantee good judgment. We need to grow up a lot more as a society before we are ready to play with the new toys being so efficiently made for us by the precocious scientists."

"Precocious scientists" may indeed be playing on our vanities and self-indulgences, but what about the therapeutic potential—the chance to heal human ills—that resides within the new genetics? Nuclear transfer technology may lead to human reproductive cloning, but it is also the best means we have of producing enough of the undifferentiated stem cells to eventually cure a wide range of diseases and disabilities. Genetic manipulation may lead to a race of elitist, self-designed posthumans, but it also contains the seeds of the genetic identification and prevention of a vast array of medical and systemic human afflictions.

As with any number of new technologies, the genetic revolution presents us with what is known as the slippery slope—the dilemma of how to make optimum use of what the technology has to offer and to truly maximize its benefits to society without going too far.

Perhaps the last word on the page in the ongoing debate should go to the vocal and challenging James Watson, the co-discoverer of the structure of DNA and a strong advocate of putting the fruits of the genetic revolution to work as quickly as possible.

"I can sense," Watson said recently, summing up his point of view in an informal address before a group of fellow scientists, "the tide is changed, and genetic manipulation will be more and more accepted. A lot of people don't want the world to be changed, but we shouldn't be too upset. We just have to go on with our business. We want to make the world better. There are people who say, well, we're playing God. I have a straightforward answer—if we don't play God, who will?"

Notes

Foreword
p. 7, In His Image . . . Gina Kolata, *Clone*, pp. 93–119.
p. 9, "a hoax and a fraud" . . . Ibid., p. 118.
p. 11, "It's unbelievable" . . . Ibid., p. 37.

Chapter 1
p. 14, partial success with frogs . . . Arlene Judith Klotzko, ed., *Cloning Sourcebook*, p. 285.
p. 14, "Cloning animals from adult cells" . . . Gina Kolata, *Clone*, p. 208.
p. 15, "A researcher working under a high-power microscope" . . . Ian Wilmut, "Cloning for Medicine," *Scientific American*, December 1998.
p. 16, low success rate . . . Arlene Judith Klotzko, ed., *Cloning Sourcebook*, p. 16.
p. 16, would be "offensive" . . . Gina Kolata, *Clone*, p. 4.
p. 18, trick the adult cell's DNA . . . Arlene Judith Klotzko, ed., *Cloning Sourcebook*, p. 122.

p. 22, Bulfield replied. . . Ibid, p. 24.

p. 22, Wilmut and Campbell . . . Ibid.

p. 23, "1000 eggs and 20 to 50 surrogate mothers" . . . Ibid, *Cloning Sourcebook*, p. 3.

Chapter 2

pp. 24–25, Kenneth M. Boyd . . . Arlene Judith Klotzo, ed., *Cloning Sourcebook*, p. 94.

p. 25, "mind-bogglingly fascinating" . . . Ibid., p. 163.

p. 25, "quite like to be cloned" . . . Martha C. Nussbaum, ed., *Clones and Clones*, p. 55.

p. 26, "onus is on those" . . . Nussbaum, p. 66.

p. 29, Lee Silver . . . Arlene Judith Klotzko, ed., *Cloning Sourcebook*, p. 61.

p. 33, "Certainly not in any of our lifetimes" . . . Gina Kolata, *Clone*, p. 104.

p. 34, "If we don't play God" . . . Arlene Judith Klotzko, ed., *Cloning Sourcebook*, p. 20.

p. 35, Tom Harkin . . . M. L. Rantala, *Cloning, For and Against*, pp. 116–118.

p. 35, "As long as science is done ethically and openly" . . . Ibid.

p. 36, God supports cloning . . . Ibid., p. 150.

p. 37, Clonaid . . . Ibid. (accessed Feb. 26, 2004).

p. 37, "allow us to truly live forever" . . . www.Clonaid.com

p. 39, In October 2004, Boisselier announced. . . Ibid. (accessed March 25, 2005).

Chapter 3

p. 40, "Repugnant" . . . Arlene Judith Klotzko, ed., *Cloning Sourcebook*, p. 63.

p. 40, 90 percent of those questioned . . . *Time*, March 10, 1997.

p. 42, Arthur L. Caplan . . . Arlene Judith Klotzko, ed., *Cloning Sourcebook*, p 158.

p. 46, "Cloning is inherently despotic" . . . Glenn McGee, ed., *Human Cloning Debate*, p. 96.

p. 50, "GenRich class and the Natural class" . . . Lee Silver, Remaking Eden, p. 7.

p. 53, "arrogance of Western science" . . . Glenn McGee, ed., *Human Cloning Debate*, p. 293.

p. 55, "ban on human cloning" . . . David G. Kirkpatrick, "Bush Assures Evangelicals . . . ," *The New York Times*, March 12, 2004.

Chapter 4

p. 56, "I'm not saying it's good" . . . Laurie Goodstein and Denise Grady, "Split on Clones of Embryos . . . ," *The New York Times*, February 13, 2004.

p. 59, Rats that had been paralyzed . . . www.newscientist.com/hottopics/cloning (accessed Sept. 10, 2003).

p. 59, treating damaged mouse hearts with stem cells . . . www.nz herald.co.nz/story display (accessed Feb. 11, 2004).

p. 61, "nothing . . . without reasonable risk" . . . Jerome Groopman, "The Reeve Effect," *The New Yorker*, November 10, 2003.

p. 63, Twelve female volunteers . . . Jose B. Cibelli, Robert P. Lanza, and Michael D. West, "The First Human Cloned Embryo," *Scientific American*, January 2002.

p. 65, "ended up with 30 blastocysts" . . . Gina Kolata, "Cloning Creates Human Embryos," *The New York Times*, Feb. 12, 2004.

p. 66, "cloned blastocysts for babymaking" . . . Ibid.

p. 67, "cell populations . . . must be pure" . . . Andrew Pollack, "Medical and Ethical Issues Cloud Cloning for Therapy," *The New York Times*, February 13, 2004.

p. 68, Can Nasal Stem Cells Repair Spinal Injuries? . . . Innovation: Miracle Cell," PBS, April 13, 2004.

p. 69, "treated with a transplant of umbilical cord blood . . ." Ibid.

Chapter 5

pp. 72–73, Jesse Gelsinger . . . Sheryl Gay Stolberg, "The Biotech Death of Jesse Gelsinger," *The New York Times Sunday Magazine*, Nov. 28, 1999.

p. 76, manage the risks of gene therapy . . . "Signs of Progress in Gene Therapies," www.inpharma.com/news (accessed April 22, 2004).

p. 77, susceptibility gene known as BRCA1 . . . PBS, DNA Series, *Curing Cancer*, 2003.

p. 78, "serious diseases no child should be born with" . . . PBS, DNA Series, *Pandora's Box*, 2003.

p. 80, "start with a fertilized embryo" . . . Bill McKibben, *Enough*, p. 10.

p. 81, "lifelong resistance to . . . AIDS" . . . Silver, *Remaking Eden*, p. 3.

p. 83, "state-of-the-art gene job" . . . McKibben, *Enough*, p. 34.

p. 84, "accelerate endlessly and unstoppably" . . . Ibid., p. 35.

p. 84, "confuse our role with God's" . . . Michael J. Sandel, "The Case Against Perfection," *The Atlantic Monthly*, April 2004.

p. 84, "school for humility" . . . Ibid.

Chapter 6

p. 87, "pig cells that were coated with human proteins" . . . Gina Kolata, *Clone*, p. 9.

p. 88, "food from cloned animals" . . . Andrew Pollack, "F.D.A. Finds Cloned Animals Safe for Food," *The New York Times*, October 31, 2003.

p. 91, collected skin cells from a gaur . . . Robert P. Lanza, Betsy L. Dresser, and Philip Damiani, "Cloning Noah's Ark," *Scientific American*, November 2000.

p. 93, "Cells taken from cloned mouse embryos" . . . news.bbc.co.uk/2/hi/health/3123978.stm (accessed Feb. 23, 2004).

pp. 93–94, nerve cell from a mouse's nose . . .

www.hum-molgen.de/NewsGen/02-2004
(accessed Feb. 23, 2004).

p. 94, egg from the mother monkey and sperm from . . .
www.accessexcellence.org/
WN/SUA 14/monkeybiz (accessed Feb. 23, 2004).

p. 95, "used 285 eggs to get three live clones" . . .
www.bbc.co.uk/1/hi/sci/tech/329107 (accessed Feb. 23, 2004).

p. 97, litter of five transgenic piglets . . .
www.bbc.co.uk/1/hi/sci/tech/1272625 (accessed Feb. 11, 2004).

p. 98, clone a pet dog named Missy . . . Arlene Judith
Klotzko, ed., *Cloning Sourcebook*, p. 169.

p. 98, pattern on cats' coats . . .
www.nature.com/nsu/020211 (accessed Feb. 23, 2004).

p. 100, "20 to 40 rabbits would" . . .
news.bbc.co.uk/1/hi/sci/tech/1899477
(accessed Feb. 23, 2004).

p. 100, mule born on May 4, 2003 . . . www.abc.net.au/
science/news/stories/s868113 (accessed Feb. 11, 2004).

p. 101, opposing "pet cloning because" . . .
www.hsus.org/ace/13214 (accessed Feb. 23, 2004).

p. 102, skin cell from a Haflinger mare . . .
www.washingtonpost.com/ac2/wp-dyn/A23350-2003
Aug6 (accessed Feb. 11, 2004)

p. 103, an expert in horse genetics . . . Andrew Pollack,
"Another Milestone of Cloning . . . ," *The New York
Times*, May 30, 2003.

p. 104, stabilize the rat eggs . . . news.bbc.co.uk/2/hi/
science/nature/3136776 (accessed Feb. 11, 2004).

p. 105, "Pain is pain, no matter what the species" . . .
Arlene Judith Klotzko, ed., *Cloning Sourcebook*, p.160.

p. 105, "degree of distress on animals" . . . Ibid., p. 167.

p. 107, "ethical obligations we have to nonhuman
animals" . . . Ibid.

Chapter 7

p. 109, "*Homo Sapiens* is not the final word" . . .
Gregory Stock, *Redesigning Humans*, p. 1.

p. 109, Auxiliary chromosomes . . . Ibid., p. 67.

p. 110, "leaping across thresholds" . . . Bill McKibben, *Enough*, p. 118.

p. 110, "A sixth of the American population" . . . Ibid., p. 37.

p 111, "opportunities . . . outweigh the risks" . . . Gregory Stock, *Redesigning Humans*, p. 201.

p. 111, "rejiggered cells" . . . Bill McKibben, p. 199.

p. 111, "Once we start down the path" . . . McKibben, p. 210.

pp. 111, 113, "brutal decay is the fate in store" . . . Gregory Stock, *Redesigning Humans*, p. 78.

p. 113, life spans of . . . roundworms . . . McKibben, *Enough*, p. 152.

p. 114, "a stage before they are completely developed" . . . Stanley Shostak, p. 163.

p. 115, "wrongful immortality" . . . Ibid., p.199.

p. 116, "Objecting even slightly to immortality" . . . McKibben, pp. 156–157.

p. 116, "Death's overpowering reality" . . . Ibid., pp. 147–148.

p. 116, "immortality is a fool's goal" . . . Ibid., p. 161.

p. 117, Rael, the founder of Clonaid . . . www.clonaid.com (accessed Feb. 26, 2004).

p. 119, "biologic nonsense" . . . Glenn McGee, ed., *The Human Cloning Debate*, pp. 181–182.

p. 119, Sherwin B. Nuland . . . *How We Die*, pp. 133–134.

p.121, "precocious scientists" . . . Ibid., p. 135.

p.122, "genetic manipulation will be more and more accepted" . . . PBS, DNA Series, *Pandora's Box*, 2003.

Further Information

Books

DuPrau, Jeanne. *Cloning*. San Diego, CA: Lucent, 2000.

Goodnough, David. *The Debate over Human Cloning: A Pro/Con Issue*. Berkeley Heights, NJ: Enslow Publishers, 2003.

Leone, Bruno, ed. *Cloning*. San Diego, CA: Greenhaven Press, 2003.

Nardo, Don. *Cloning*. San Diego, CA: Lucent, 2002.

Spangenburg, Ray, and Kit Moser. *Genetic Engineering*. New York: Benchmark Books, 2004.

Yount, Lisa, ed. *Cloning*. San Diego, CA: Greenhaven Press, 2000.

Web Sites

The Clone Zone
222.bbc.co.uk/science/genes/gene_safari/clone_zone/intro.shtml

How Cloning Works
www.howstuffworks.com/cloning.htm

The Reproductive Cloning Network
www.ReproductiveCloning.net

Roslin Institute
www.ri.bbsrc.ac.uk/public/cloning.html

University of Pennsylvania Center for Bioethics
Bioethics.net

Bibliography

Andrews, Lori B. *The Clone Age: Adventures in the New World of Reproductive Technology*. New York: Henry Holt, 2000.

Klotzko, Arlene Judith, ed. *The Cloning Sourcebook*. NewYork: Oxford University Press, 2001.

Kolata, Gina B. *Clone: The Road to Dolly and the Path Ahead*. New York: Morrow, 1998.

McGee, Glenn, ed. *The Human Cloning Debate*. Berkeley, CA: Berkeley Hills Books, 2002.

McKibben, Bill. *Enough: Staying Human in an Engineered Age*. New York: Henry Holt, 2003.

Nussbaum, Martha C., and Cass R. Sunstein, eds. *Clones and Clones: Facts and Fantasies about Human Cloning*. New York: Norton, 1998.

Rantala, M. L., and Arthur J. Milgram, eds. *Cloning, For and Against*. Chicago and La Salle, IL: Open Court, 1999.

Sandel, Michael J. "The Case Against Perfection." *The Atlantic Monthly*, April 2004.

Scientific American, eds. *Understanding Cloning*. New York: Warner Books, 2002.

Shostak, Stanley. *Becoming Immortal: Combining Cloning and Stem-Cell Therapy*. Albany: State University of New York Press, 2002.

Silver, Lee M. *Remaking Eden: Cloning and Beyond in a Brave New World*. New York: Avon, 1997.

Stock, Gregory. *Redesigning Humans: Our Inevitable Genetic Future*. New York: Houghton Mifflin, 2002.

Index

Page numbers in **boldface** are illustrations.

About the Author

Lila Perl has published more than fifty books for young people and adults, including fiction and nonfiction. Her nonfiction writings have been mainly in the fields of social history, family memoir, and biography. She has traveled extensively to do cultural and background studies of seven African countries, as well as China, Puerto Rico, Guatemala, and Mexico. She has written on subjects as diverse as foods and food customs, geneology, Egyptian mummies, Latino popular culture, and the Holocaust.

Two of her books have been honored with American Library Association Notable awards: *Red-Flannel Hash* and *Shoo-Fly Pie* and *Four Perfect Pebbles*. Ten titles have been selected as Notable Children's Trade Books in the field of Social Studies. Lila Perl has also received a Boston Globe Horn Book award, a Sidney Taylor Committee award, and a Young Adults' Choice award from the International Reading Association. The New York Public Library has cited her work among Best Books for the Teen Age. Her most recent book for Marshall Cavendish Benchmark was *Terrorism*, in our Open for Debate series.

Lila Perl lives in Beechhurst, New York.